CONTENTS

TIBET
TURNING THE WHEEL OF LIFE
Françoise Pommaret

Thames & Hudson

What do we mean when we talk about Tibet? The Tibet of Tibetans in exile? The Tibet of Tibetan culture? Tibet as a geographical entity? Or Tibet as defined by the People's Republic of China? In 1959, a call to resistance that appeared in *The Tibet Mirror* was addressed not to Tibetans, but to 'all *tsampa*-eaters', so closely is this staple food of roast barley flour associated with the identity of Tibet. But this shorthand description gives little hint of the complex reality and land that lie behind it.

CHAPTER 1
LAND AND IDENTITY

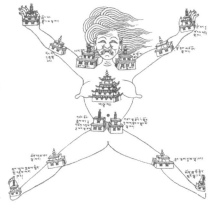

Multicoloured prayer flags and white scarves are everywhere in Tibet (opposite), streaming above mountain tops and holy sites. Tibet's conversion to Buddhism is represented in this drawing of a female demon (right), symbolizing the country, with temples placed on her heart and joints, pinning her to the ground and subduing her.

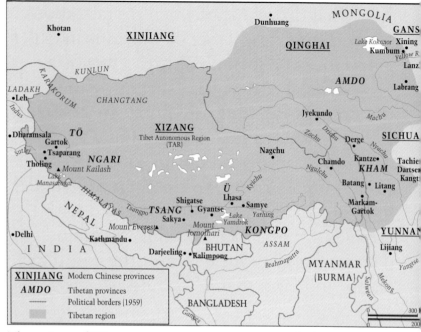

The regions of Tibet

The area called 'Tibet' is a shifting one, varying according to the standpoint taken – ethnic or cultural, historical or contemporary – which is why the few statistics that are available should be treated with caution. It would therefore be helpful at this point to specify the different accepted meanings of the term, and to define the one that will be used in this book.

The Tibetan sphere of influence covers an immense area, stretching from Ladakh in the west to Mongolia in the north and Nepal and Bhutan in the south. Some of these regions, though subject in varying degrees to Tibetan religious and cultural influences, no longer form part of Tibet. A few areas, such as Bhutan and Mongolia, have now gained their independence. In most cases, however, these regions now belong to other nations: Ladakh, Zanskar, Spiti, Lahaul, North Kinnaur, Sikkim and northern Arunachal Pradesh are all Indian; Mugu,

The map above shows the extent of the Tibetan cultural region presently occupied by China, giving the traditional Tibetan names of the provinces and the Chinese names. Tibet consists of a high plateau (at an altitude of about 4,000 m) criss-crossed and surrounded by mountain ranges (rising to 6,000 m). To the south and west lie the Himalayas, to the north the Kunlun, and to the east the Bayan Khara. Neighbouring countries are reached through gorges and mountain passes.

Dolpo, Manang, Yolmo/Helambu, Sherpa territory and northern Arun, meanwhile, are Nepalese.

Though smaller in area, the ethnic and cultural region of Tibet still covers some 3,800,000 km², or an area about the size of western Europe, containing a Tibetan population of just over six million. Making up one third of the surface area of modern-day China (9,600,000 km²), it represents a mere 0.46 per cent of its total population. Within this area, the great provinces of Amdo and Kham (in the north-east and east respectively), U-Tsang (in the centre) and Ngari (in the west) are subdivided into smaller regions, many with their own separate histories, such as Dagpo, Kongpo, Lhodrak, Powo, Derge, Nangchen, Gyalrong, Nyarong, Gyalthang, Trehor and Guge.

It is impossible to speak of the historic kingdom of Tibet in absolute terms, as its frontiers have shifted over the centuries. Stretching as far as Dunhuang on the Silk Road and northern Yunnan, it embraced Ladakh and parts of northern India and Nepal in the 8th century, but by the early 20th century reached its eastern limits at the Yangtse River. But a historic Tibet does not exist outside of specific timeframes. The Chinese language contains no word to designate ethnic Tibet, and similarly, Tibetan has no single term to cover the concept of 'Han China and Tibet'. The Chinese name for China, *Zhongguo* or 'land of the centre', does not include Tibet, and the Tibetans know China by the name of *Gyanak*, or 'black expanse'.

As far as the Tibetan government – in exile since 1959 – is concerned, the name Tibet indicates the whole of the ethnic and cultural region of Tibet, as designated by the term *Bod cholkha sum* –'Tibet of the three provinces': U-Tsang, Kham and Amdo. When using the name Tibet

Chortens (*stupa* in Sanskrit) dot the landscape, reliquary monuments which may be commemorative or protective: those pictured below are at the monastery of Maochok in Lhodrak, at 4,200 m. Varying slightly in shape from region to region, chortens symbolize the mind of the Buddha, and are of course sacred. Like prayer flags, they have come to symbolize an aspect of the Tibetan national identity. The relationship between this identity and Buddhism is today ambiguous and complex. In the wake of the Chinese occupation and the exile of some of the population, Buddhism has become a manifestation of national feeling – not so much a religion, in the strict sense, as a political declaration and form of protest.

in its general ethnic and cultural sense, scholars and specialists often add the name of the Tibetan province in question, along with its present-day Chinese name.

In China today, the name for Tibet (*Xizang*, or 'western treasure house') is applied solely to the Tibetan Autonomous Region (TAR, created in 1965), with Lhasa as its capital. Its 1,200,000 km² extent covers the provinces of U-Tsang and Ngari, as well as western Kham, with its capital Chamdo. The dismemberment of the rest of Greater Tibet started in the early 18th century, with part of the province of Amdo. In the early 20th century, part of Kham became nominally a province called Xikang, which was abolished by the Communists in 1955. Today, the province of Amdo is divided between three Chinese provinces, Qinghai, Gansu and Sichuan, while Kham is split between Sichuan, Yunnan and the TAR. For the sake of convenience and unless otherwise stated, the name Tibet is used here in the sense of the ethnic and cultural region of Tibet.

The name of Tibet

As is so often the case, Tibet has been known by different names to different cultures. The Western name, Tibet, comes from the Arabic *Tübbet/Tubbat*, which itself derives from *Töpän/Töput*, the name used in the Turco-Mongolian dialect of the Tuyuhun peoples with whom the Arabs had established contacts.

Tibetan script (shown here in a Buddhist manuscript in 'printed' script, from Kachu in central Tibet) is derived from an Indian written language of the 7th century. It is a syllabary using thirty consonants and five vowels. Used for a monosyllabic language with intonations, it has become a complex script which can differentiate between words with similar pronunciations but different spellings. Certain consonants are combined to give different sounds, such as *zl*, pronounced *d*, and are placed as subscripts or before or after the stem consonant in order to differentiate between words. For example, *lha*, *la* and *bla* are all pronounced 'la', but mean 'god', 'pass' and 'soul' respectively. The script is read from left to right, and has no capitals, punctuation or paragraphs, and one word may be made up of two monosyllables. As well as 'printed' script there are also cursive scripts. Books are either written by hand or printed using carved wooden blocks.

The Chinese describe ancient Tibet as the *Tufan* or *Tubo* empire. The Tibetans themselves call their country *Bö* or *Bod*, a name which has two different meanings, according to the context in which it is used. Between Tibetans, it is generally used to indicate central Tibet, with the western provinces of Kham and Amdo known

Tibetan women are hardworking and tough. Even when herding, they continue to spin wool (below), and in legends the spindle is traditionally

by the separate name of *Dokham*. Yet this popular internal usage does not however mean that in a broader context the people of Kham and Amdo do not consider themselves as *Böpa*, or Tibetans. Thus in Amdo and Kham, the term *Gya Bö nyi*, or 'both China and Tibet', implies that both provinces form part of Bö, or Tibet. In relation to foreigners, and especially to the Chinese, all Tibetans consider themselves *Böpa*, or 'people of Bö'. Today the slogan *Bö gi rang-tsen* means 'Tibetan independence', Bö here signifying Tibet in the ethnic and cultural sense. Indeed, as early as the imperial era,

used as a female symbol. Traditional headdresses have disappeared in central Tibet, but are still seen in eastern Tibet, where they serve to identify families or tribal groups (opposite below). Beads of coral, amber and turquoise, which is associated with the soul, are prized by both men and women.

Bö was the name used to describe the country as a whole, as attested by the bilingual stele commemorating the treaty agreed between China and Tibet in 821–22, which stands in front of the Jokhang temple in Lhasa.

Geographical and ecological diversity

Most of Tibet consists of the bed of the sea of Tethys, which dried up 100 million years ago, leaving behind it the numerous saltwater lakes scattered across the country today. To the south, the Tibetan plateau is bordered by the sweeping curve of the Himalayas which, from the Karakoram to northern Burma, separates it from the Indian subcontinent. To the west, it abuts the junction of the Karakoram and Himalayas, while to the east it

Contrary to the popular image of Tibet as a barren plateau, the country contains many different landscapes, changing with altitude. The zone of human habitation rises from 2,800 to 5,300 m. South-eastern and eastern Tibet is characterized by deep, fertile valleys surrounded by mountains. The sloping roofs of the houses in these regions are an indication of the

rises into the mountains of the Amnye Machen, Bayan Khara, Mynak Konga and Minshan ranges. To the north and north-west, the plateau is cut off from Central Asia by the Kunlun Shan mountains and the Qaidam depression, while opening out into the plains of Amdo around Lake Kokonor. The plateau itself is crisscrossed by several mountain ranges rising to over 6,000 m, the largest of which are the Transhimalayas and the Nyanchen Thangla.

All the great rivers of Asia rise in Tibet, and have their own names in Tibetan: the Mekong, Yangtse, Yellow River, Irrawaddy, Salween and Brahmaputra (Tsangpo) all run through central Tibet, while the Indus and Sutlej cross mountain ranges through spectacular gorges before

high levels of rainfall (as in the Gyalrong region in eastern Tibet, above left). In the drier climate of central and western Tibet, the landscape is more austere, with bare mountains flanking broad valleys that are fertile only close to rivers and at altitudes below 4,200 m. Here, villages are often built on the fringes of high-altitude oases (above right), where barley and rape can be grown.

winding across the plains of India and China to flow into the China Sea, the Arabian Sea or the Indian Ocean.

Tibet is not, as is commonly believed, merely an arid, desolate plateau. In most of the country, the altitude at which its people live ranges from 3,100 to 5,000 m, it is true, and nights on the windswept plateau are cold, though the days are very sunny. The region of Changtang in the west and north-west is particularly inhospitable. But in the east and south-east, the monsoon rains manage to cross the barrier of the Himalayas and the eastern mountain ranges, and in the warmer and damper climate, both coniferous and deciduous forests thrive. The north-east is a region of immense pastures and rolling hills at an altitude of

Above 4,200 m is the domain of sheep, goats and yaks, which in summer climb with their shepherds and goatherds to pastures as high as 5,300 m, as at Markyang in the Nyemo region to the west of Lhasa (left). Above 5,300 m is a barren, rocky world where snow may fall throughout the year. Inhabited only by deer, snow leopards and birds of prey, this is the realm of the mountain

4,000 m. Barley is the most widespread crop, but wheat and rape are also grown, and the lowest-lying areas support orchards. As well as serving as beasts of burden, yaks are an indispensable source of both food and materials: even their dung is used as fuel for fires. In the west, wild goats graze the meagre pastures, while the hills of the north-east are the domain of wild sheep.

The origins of the Tibetan people

The Tibetans have a number of different creation myths. According to one of the earliest, dating back to a pre-Buddhist religion, the creator god sent his son to earth to create the human race. There he coupled with a female demon, and the offspring of their union gave rise to the

gods that reign over the wellbeing and prosperity of their territory in return for the respect and veneration shown to them by humans. Peaks above 6,000 m are permanently snow-covered in a mineral world of breathtaking monochrome beauty (right, looking south from Maochok to the 7,300-m peaks of the Tibet-Bhutan border).

six original Tibetan tribes. The most widely believed version, however, is a much more recent Buddhist myth, dating from the 12th century, in which the Tibetans were born of the union of the bodhisattva Avalokiteshvara and a female rock demon, so inheriting the compassion of their paternal ancestor and the ferocity of their maternal one.

But however interesting they may be, these myths cannot make up for the lack of precise scientific data which only genetic testing could yield. Even today, the origins of the Tibetan people remain largely unknown. Theories based on anthropological observations and archaeological discoveries tend to favour multiple origins, with a dominant substratum of Mongol blood.

The extensive racial intermixing and assimilation of foreign peoples (including Turco-Mongols such as the Sumpa and Tuyuhun, the Indo-Scythians, and later the Mongols of Zhang Zhung), which started in the time of the Tibetan empire in the 7th to 9th centuries and continued in later eras, is

evidence of racial diversity throughout history. The exception to this would seem to be eastern Tibet, where western and Chinese analysts today tend to believe the inhabitants are descended from the Qiang tribes. The existence of these Tibetan-Burmese peoples in northern China is documented as early as the Zhou period (1121–222 BC), and they later migrated to the region around Lake Kokonor and to present-day Sichuan, where some of their descendants may still be found. These people share the Tibetan belief of their descent from a monkey, and their use of a white sheep as a sacrificial animal.

While it is not possible to trace the precise origins of the inhabitants of Tibet, the layering of different peoples and the fluidity of their movements bear witness – despite the commonly held views to the contrary – to the accessibility of this region from earliest history. From the 7th century AD, Chinese chronicles refer to the existence of a people called the *Tufan*.

A shared sense of place?

What unites the Tibetan people is their shared culture, marks of identity which transcend differences of dialect and dress or traditional sources of dispute. Characteristic of the whole of Tibet, from the desolate western plateau to the forests of the east, these markers – despite local differences – are sufficiently distinctive to recognized as Tibetan.

What form do they take? First and foremost, they may be seen in the form of a physical stamp on the landscape, rendering it instantly identifiable as Tibetan: prayer scarves streaming in the wind, chortens dotting the roads, cairns marking the summits of mountain passes, and sanctuaries dedicated to local divinities clinging to rocky mountainsides or built against house walls. Houses and villages conform to a common model, based on a strong conception of the opposition of the lower valleys, as cultivated and civilized, and the upper valleys, as

The Tibetan national identity is rooted partly in myths and traditional ways of representing the world. Opposite, a modern painting depicts the three worlds over which three different types of deity reign: *lou* who rule the underworld, seas and lakes; *tsen*, the fierce warriors who rule over the earth; and the benign *lha* of the celestial realm. Above, a Tibetan creation myth is illustrated in a painting from the Norbulingka Institute, Lhasa. In a cave near the town of Tsetang, a monkey, the spiritual emanation of Avalokiteshvara, and a female demon sit surrounded by their children, ancestors of the Tibetans, who derive their spirituality from their paternal forebear and their ferocity from their maternal one.

untamed or wild. The vocabulary of place is precise: *tö* indicates the uppermost part of a valley, while *me* denotes the lowest reaches. Terms used to denote space that is uninhabited and potentially dangerous all contain the word *ri*. Generally translated in the West simply as 'mountain', *ri*, carries much broader connotations in Tibetan culture. Thus *ri dag* means wild animals, *ri phag* a wild boar, and *ri ma* arid land, impossible to cultivate.

Although domestic architecture varies on the outside from region to region, according to environment and climate, the internal layout of houses remains fairly constant. The only rooms with a fixed use are the kitchen (the room in which daily life takes place), the storeroom, behind the kitchen to the north, and the family shrine. Always placed at the top of the building, this is also the room in which important guests are received. Livestock and grain stores are kept on the ground floor, while animal fodder is stored on the roof. The stove for ritual wood-burning may also be found on the roof, or in the courtyard, along with a shrine to the earth deity.

A collective memory

Tibetans share a communal heritage of myths, fragments of their history and characters from it, and

Tibetan villages (above) consist of two self-contained worlds set one within the other: the houses cluster together (except in some regions of Kham) to form 'blocks', while at the same time remaining private entities within themselves. Typically, village houses have small windows in their external walls, with larger ones looking on to an internal courtyard which provides shelter from the wind, and where fodder and livestock can be accommodated. The walls are principally of cob or stone, with wood being limited chiefly to eastern Tibet, as in Derge (opposite, below).

even of spatial representations of their land. One of the most telling illustrations of this combines all these elements. A female demon, symbolizing Tibet in its primitive state and covering the land with her body, was vanquished by King Songsten Gampo (620–49). By the method of building Buddhist temples over her heart and along her limbs, he pinned her to the ground and so prevented her from doing harm. With its profound level of symbolism, this is one of the myths that is anchored most deeply in the Tibetans' collective memory. Another myth of great resonance is that of the reign of Gesar, King of Ling.

Because it has been handed down orally, this collective memory has naturally undergone changes over the centuries; but it is also known through written texts, transcribed in a common Tibetan language which has hardly altered since it first evolved in the 7th century. Embracing the entire region, this written lingua franca has encouraged the development and diffusion of a large body of literary, religious and historical texts. Not limited to the borders of Greater Tibet, it also includes the whole area of Tibetan culture. Hence from Amdo, in north-eastern Tibet, to Ladakh, over 3,000 km away in the far west, the same texts can be read and discussed, when at the same time linguistic differences render the different dialects mutually incomprehensible in conversation.

The Tibetan saying 'Every land has its own way of speaking, every lama has his own way of teaching' shows

The principal room, and the only one warmed by a hearth or stove, is the kitchen (below), where everyone has an allotted place according to their social rank and their place in the family. Those of the lowest social standing and distant relatives sit closest to the door. All visitors are offered tea made with salted butter. The walls are blackened by smoke as chimneys are traditionally unknown in Tibet; smoke invariably fills the room, although some escapes through a hole in the roof.

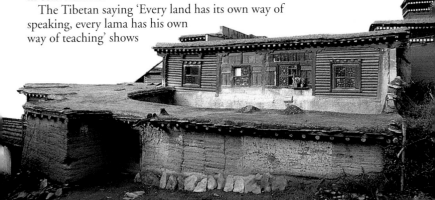

that the Tibetans are fully aware of their diversity but nevertheless feel that it is transcended by the markers of the common identity to which they all belong, to the extent of themselves adopting the epithet of 'red-faced *tsampa*-eaters'. The years of Chinese occupation have served only to deepen and sharpen this profound sense of national identity. Far from setting them in stone, the Tibetans are constantly adapting the basic elements of their cultural heritage, sometimes giving prominence to different aspects according to the requirements of the changing political or ideological context.

Shared beliefs

The shared beliefs of the Tibetans focus particularly on local divinities, including those of mountains and lakes, who ensure happiness in earthly life: these gods have their origins in pre-Buddhist beliefs. With their markedly anthropomorphic natures, the deities may be beneficent or wrathful according to the manner in which humans comport themselves in society and in their natural environment. Highly irascible, these gods are liable to vent their anger in the form of hailstorms or by causing the death of livestock, while at the same time squabbling jealously with each other over the occupancy of springs or other natural riches. Each has his or

her favourite foods and chosen partner, and none of them shows any hesitation in being unfaithful or in forsaking their region for warmer climes in winter. They are worshipped in a fairly similar fashion throughout Tibet, with incense burning, offerings of food, alcohol or milk, modest propitiation ceremonies, and occasionally horse races and archery or shooting contests.

Buddhism is viewed by many, especially in the West, as one of the main components, if not the sole component, of the identity of Tibet. Certainly Buddhism is an important factor in Tibet, especially since so many

Mount Kailash (also called Gang Tise or Gang Rinpoche – 'precious mountain' in Tibetan) lies in western Tibet. Standing 6,638 m tall, it is believed to be the central pillar of the universe and the centre of the cosmic mandala. The Indus, Sutlej, Brahmaputra and Karnali rivers all have their source close to this peak, which dominates the Tibetan plateau. A pilgrimage around the mountain – home of Shiva or Chakrasamvara, and sacred to Buddhists, Bönpo, Hindus and Jains alike – is an act of purification. It generally takes three days, but the hardiest souls complete it in twenty hours, prostrating themselves as they go. The pilgrimage is punctuated by prayers and prostrations at sites of symbolic significance, and the journey through the Drolma pass, 5,650 m high, is viewed as a rebirth.

Buddhism, which became the state religion in the 8th century, has undergone changes over the centuries, assimilating native beliefs and evolving the distinctive philosophical and liturgical features that define it today. It is known by various names, including Tibetan Buddhism, *Vajrayana* (the 'diamond vehicle'), Tantric Buddhism and – particularly in the early 20th century – Lamaism. The Tibetan word *chö*, which originally meant 'religion' or 'system of beliefs', has become synonymous with Buddhism. The burning of branches of juniper or pine (*sang* in Tibetan) on mountain tops or rooftops, is a local purification ritual that has been assimilated by Buddhism (left).

•With this essence of the forests of the high mountains, sweet-smelling and duly prepared incense, let us purify the gods above, let us purify the *lou* spirits of the underworld, let us purify the *nyen* spirits of the space between, let us purify our homes, our clothes and our possessions.•

Sang ritual prayer

Buddhists in exile have found unity around the charismatic figure of the 14th Dalai Lama, but the ten per cent of the population who are not Buddhists but Bönpo are undeniably Tibetans, as are the few thousand Tibetan Muslims. Buddhism is fundamental to Tibetan society, but the identity of Tibet cannot be reduced to Buddhism alone.

For most Westerners, the name Tibet means Buddhism and lamas. This image, propagated by many books, is largely true but at the same time should be tempered with an understanding of the specific – and sometimes surprising – philosophical, symbolic and iconographic characteristics of this faith. A product of Tibetan culture, Tibetan Buddhism can be disconcerting both for 'rationalist' Westerners and followers of a 'simpler' form of Buddhism.

CHAPTER 2

RELIGIONS AND BELIEFS

Karma is the result of past actions, and leads to rebirth as illustrated by the great Wheel of Life (opposite). Ignorance, anger and desire are original poisons, symbolized in the centre of the wheel by three animals: the pig, the serpent and the cock. The poisons make human beings fall back into the cycle of incarnations – *samsara* – and hence into suffering. The ultimate goal of sentient beings is to leave the circle and attain Enlightenment. There are several different ways of doing this: to enter into holy orders, to go on a pilgrimage, or to meditate. One of the simplest is to turn the prayer wheel (left).

The pre-Buddhist belief system of ancient Tibet

The Tibet in which Buddhism arrived in the 7th century was by no means devoid of religious beliefs. Indeed, there existed a deeply rooted system of beliefs which

was partly assimilated and partly obliterated by Buddhism, with Buddhist missionaries even penning virtual manuals of conversion techniques, examples of which have been found in manuscripts discovered in the Dunhuang caves. Our understanding of this religion, known as Bön, remains incomplete. Only a painstaking reading of the fragmentary Dunhuang manuscripts could produce a contemporary portrait of the period when this faith was dominant, the days of the Tibetan empire. Archaeological excavations are still too few, and the study of pre-Buddhist sites and monuments is far from systematic. All the same, it is now possible to discern the broad outlines of this ancient religion. The Bön universe was created by the pcha gods, who lived in the sky, imposed order and delegated powers to their representatives on earth. The

Ancient Tibetan beliefs were organized into a religious system that was probably named Bön, and the priests were named Bönpo. Many Westerners long regarded this faith as nothing but sorcery and witchcraft, but from the 1960s onwards, scholars began to reject this negative interpretation after studying the Dunhuang manuscripts. Above, a deity protecting a territory; on both pages, animals that ferry souls to the land of the dead.

earth was held in place by the mountains, which stretched out the sky like a tent. When humans died, they were guided by animals such as sheep, horses and yaks to the land of the dead. This consisted of a region of suffering and a region of happiness, where, surrounded by their possessions and food, the dead awaited resurrection in a new golden age.

Ages of prosperity and times of calamity followed one another, corresponding to periods when the faith was flourishing or was persecuted.

Priests, known as *bönpo* or *shen*, practised numerous rituals, including animal sacrifice, in order to appease a multitude of divinities who were very closely linked with nature. These gods might be benevolent or wrathful to humans, depending on the manner in which the latter comported themselves. The two most important categories of gods appear to have been mountain gods – the *kula* and the female *mamo* – who protected the lives and power of nobles and the king. Safeguarding stability and order, they brought good health and abundant harvests and livestock. When angered they would abandon the king, causing his death and endangering the stability of his kingdom and the prosperity of his subjects. Major rituals were therefore necessary to appease these life-supporting gods.

Royalty was sacred, as kings were descended from the first king of the creation myths, a *pcha* sky god, who chose to manifest himself on earth in Tibet because it was high and pure. Divination, using a variety of techniques, played an important practical role, dictating important decisions at both a state and domestic level. This highly anthropomorphic religion possessed a rich

The term Bön also refers to a religious school established in the 11th century in Zhang Zhung in western Tibet, and known as Yungdrung Bön. Its founding master was Tönpa Shenrab, the equivalent of the Buddha Shakyamuni for the Buddhists, but to date there is no documentary evidence of his existence. The term *yungdrung* denotes

the swastika, a Bön symbol. Bön rituals and teachings have retained some elements of the pre-Buddhist faith, but the philosophy is close to that of the Buddhist Nyingmapa school. Above, Bön tantrists in Amdo, performing a ritual with little drums.

mythology which served to bring meaning to its rituals. These myths and rituals were both passed down in part to the Yungdrung Bön school of faith, which came into being from the 11th century.

The origins of Buddhism

Buddhism arrived in Tibet in the 7th century, simultaneously from China and from India, each of these sources offering a different approach to the attainment of Enlightenment. In the Chinese Ch'an doctrine (later Zen in Japan), or 'sudden way', mental or physical activity was an obstacle to Enlightenment, whereas in the Indian *Madhyamaka*, the 'Middle Way', Enlightenment was attained through virtuous actions and assiduous religious practice. According to Tibetan historiography, in the 8th century a great debate took place between these two schools at Samye Monastery. Whatever the form and the reality of this debate, controversy raged, with the Indian 'Middle Way' emerging triumphant, but incorporating elements of Tantrism.

Tantrism is a religious movement which plays a prominent part in both Hinduism and Buddhism. It lays stress on the practice of yoga, on secret teachings founded on texts known as Tantra, which can be understood only when explained by a master or guru, and finally – for its most advanced followers – on sexual symbolism. At this period, it was practised particularly in north-eastern India, Swat (present-day

In India, in 'Greater Vehicle' Buddhism (*Mahayana*) which was prevalent at the time, 'the way of the tantras' (*Tantrayana*) coexisted with 'the middle way' (*Madhyamaka*). The 'great fulfilled', such as Dombi Heruka, seen below with his consort (17th-century painting) were important in their role of passing on the tantra texts to the Tibetan people.

Pakistan) and Kashmir. It was from Swat that Padmasambhava emerged in the 8th century. This Tantric master, of whose life we know very little, was to become a religious hero throughout the Tibetan world, with a golden legend growing up around him from the 12th century.

The Tibetans view India as the cradle of their religion, with many of the faithful making the long journey to spend months or years at the feet of Indian masters in Indian monasteries (it is this aspect of Tibetan Buddhism, incidentally, which enables the Chinese government today to describe it as a 'foreign' religion, imported from abroad). This tradition was interrupted only in the early 13th century, when Muslim invaders destroyed monasteries throughout northern India.

Tibetan Buddhism

Buddhism gradually adapted itself to and imposed itself upon this substratum of an indigenous religion whose beliefs were impossible to reconcile with its own, which were based on non-creation, impermanence and karma, and the importance of actions. While it assimilated several elements, such as local divinities, Buddhism gradually abolished or adapted the more troublesome aspects, such as the myth of creation, animal sacrifices, the attainment of happiness after death, and the importance accorded to earthly life. This was nevertheless a slow process, which probably lasted from the 7th to the 10th century, and it was not accomplished without conflict. As late as the 10th century, for instance, the king of western Tibet, Yeshe Ö, criticized Buddhists who were continuing to practise animal sacrifice.

Padmasambhava – or Guru Rinpoche, 'the Precious Master' – is considered by the Nyingmapa school to be the second Buddha, and he is the subject of a 'golden legend'. This

tantrist master, originally from Swat, introduced the use of the ritual dagger (*phurba*), and he is also credited with other teachings intended to subdue hostile spirits. There are many iconographic images of him that make references to his great deeds, either real or imagined; masked dances are also dedicated to him.

In the 8th and 9th centuries, during the period known as the 'first diffusion' or 'first propagation', encouraged by the kings Senaleg and Relpachen, Tibetan Buddhists accomplished an extraordinary feat in the field of vocabulary, either designating Buddhist meanings for terms used to refer to a different concept in the pre-Buddhist religion, or creating Tibetan neologisms as translations for Buddhist terms in Sanskrit. They also compiled the *Mahavyutpatti*, the great Sanskrit-Tibetan dictionary, and laid down the rules of translation in its introduction.

Schools of Tibetan Buddhism

Tibetan Buddhism is today divided into four great schools, some of which are further subdivided into separate smaller branches. The doctrinal differences between these schools are minor, and they all possess the same fundamental beliefs. They are differentiated, however, by the importance that they place on specific texts, and in particular by the way in which complex texts are interpreted through the oral teachings of a spiritual master.

Furthermore, only those who have received this oral interpretation, under certain specified conditions, can go on to transmit it to other disciples. The teacher, or lama, is therefore a supremely important figure, since religious schools grow up around the charismatic personality and

The text of the *Prajnaparamita* Sutra – Transcendental Wisdom – is one of the most important in Buddhism. Tibetan versions may be richly illuminated, like the manuscript below, which depicts Maitreya, the Buddha of the

teachings of an individual holy man.

The school of the Nyingmapa, or 'the Ancients', follows the teachings of Padmasambhava and shares the

future, and a bodhisattva, surrounded by monks (13th–14th century, western Tibet).

philosophy of *dzogchen*, or 'great perfection', with the Bön faith. This school, which is particularly influential in central and eastern Tibet, is subdivided into a number of different religious lineages – Kathok, Dzogchen, Jangter, Peling and Tersar – whose teachers have always maintained a spiritual interaction. The Nyingmapa school follows a large body of tantra texts, translated or developed during the first diffusion of Buddhism but not recognized as valid by the other schools. From the 10th century, by contrast, all schools accepted the tantras translated or transmitted by Tibetan masters including Rinchen Zangpo.

The school of the Kadampa, or 'those bound together by oral teachings', was the first to make its appearance during the second diffusion of Buddhism. Its founder was Dromtönpa, disciple of the Indian master Atisha (982–1054), who had been invited to Tibet by the king of western Tibet in order to spread the Buddhist religion. The emphasis in this school was placed on discipline and philosophy, with the teaching of esoteric tantras reserved for an elite few. With its principal monastery at Reting (founded 1073), the school was absorbed into the Gelugpa school in the 14th century.

The exceptional work above (tempera on canvas, 19th century) illustrates one of the most complex aspects of Tibetan Buddhism. It shows offerings being made in order to please the indigenous deity Begtse, who had become the protector of Buddhism and, in particular, of the Dalai Lamas. Begtse is depicted as a ferocious warrior, here surrounded by offerings of flayed men who represent the enemies of the faith. On the tables are ritual objects, such as sacrificial cakes that have been prepared for the god. Animals both real and mythical stand guard; some are also offerings themselves.

The Sakyapa school was founded in the 9th century by the master Brogmi, who had spent eight years in the monastery at Vikramashila in India. In 1073, his pupil Könchog Gyalpo, of the Khön tribe, founded a monastery at Sakya in the province of Tsang, which gave its name to the Sakyapa school. This school was distinguished by the fact that from the outset it was led by a hierarchy from two families of the Khön tribe, who took turns in assuming this responsibility.

The Kagyupa school, the school of 'oral transmission', considered Marpa (1012–99) and his disciple, the ascetic and poet Milarepa (1052–1135), as their founders. Marpa went to study in India under the masters Naropa and Maitripa, and the esoteric practices of *The Six Yogas of Naropa* and *The Great Seal* form part of the advanced teachings of this school. The Kagyupa are subdivided into numerous branches, some of which, such as the Phagmodrupa and the Tselpa, have now disappeared, along with their oral teachings. Those that are still in existence include the Karmapa, the first school to introduce – in the 13th century – the system of hierarchical succession through a line of incarnations; the Drungpa, very active today in Ladakh; and the Drukpa, present in Bhutan since the 17th century and so closely identified with the country that they have given it its indigenous name, *Druk Yul.*

The school of the Gelugpa, or 'the Virtuous', was founded in the 14th century by the reformist monk Tsongkhapa (1357–1419). Adopting the teachings of the earlier Kadampa school, it laid stress on monastic discipline, philosophy and debate, while reserving its tantras for an elite who were reaching the end of their studies. One of their basic texts was the *Lamrin,* composed by the lama Tsongkhapa. The descendants of this school

Different Buddhist schools may place greater emphasis on the practice of yoga, or meditation, or an intensive study of the tantras or of metaphysics. However, there is nothing to prevent a follower of any school from studying in a monastery or receiving instruction from teachers of other schools, following the example of the Dalai Lamas themselves. This desire to avoid compartmentalizing the schools is epitomized by the slogan 'eclectic, not sectarian', which spread from eastern Tibet during the 19th century.

Sakya Pandita (1182–1251; left) arrived in Mongolia in 1244, at the invitation of the prince Goden, one of Genghis Khan's grandsons. Famous for its scholars, the Sakyapa school became the first to achieve political dominance in Tibet (1260–1350) after the fall of the empire in 852. In the 13th century the Jonangpa school separated from the Sakyapa. Its doctrines were regarded as heretical, and it was outlawed by the 5th Dalai Lama in the 17th century.

Paintings and statues symbolize the body of the Buddha. Some paintings are all the more sacred because they bear the hand or footprints of the holy man represented or of another famous lama. A typical example is this thangka (a painting on rolled cloth: left), which features Dromtönpa (1005–64), the Kadampa master and disciple of Atisha, who can be seen at the top of the picture (17th century).

Milarepa (below, clay statue, 15th century), committed acts of violence early in his life, then repented, and became a great thinker. He is associated with many holy sites, and is traditionally represented as emaciated, with his hand to his ear, singing his mystic poems.

Earlier Western terminology divided the Buddhist schools into 'red hats' and 'yellow hats'. This originated from Chinese classifications that date from the Qing dynasty, but does not reflect any Tibetan classification, has no religious foundation, and is rejected by the Tibetans. Opposite, a lama from the Drukpa Kagyupa school, 19th-century painting; left, Tsongkhapa, founder of the Gelugpa school, and an incarnation of Manjushri with his attributes of a sword and a book. 15th century, White Temple, Tholing.

A monk's life is strictly regulated, and the rituals are an all-absorbing activity (see overleaf). The monks are seated in a precise hierarchical order, with the youngest being closest to the entrance. Some ceremonies begin in the half-light of dawn, with the temple illuminated only by butter lamps. The atmosphere is impressive, even to non-believers. Those officiating wear heavy coats to protect themselves against the cold, but they only put on their hats at specific moments during the ceremony, and in between they keep them on their shoulders.

– dalai lamas and panchen lamas – were to assume a historical role of great importance from the 17th century onwards: in 1642, the 5th Dalai Lama assumed political power in Tibet, and the Gelugpa became the dominant political power.

Monks, lamas and nuns

Contrary to the general assumption in the West, not all lamas are monks, and not all monks are lamas, or gurus. Indeed, the word *lama* does not mean 'monk' but rather 'spiritual teacher', the word for monk being *drapa*. A monk is a Buddhist holy man who has taken vows of celibacy. In Tibetan Buddhism, this vow is obligatory for those wishing to be monks. Monks follow an educational curriculum, but do not necessarily become lamas, or spiritual teachers capable of giving guidance to others.

Monks are under the authority of an abbot, or *khenpo*. They are nonetheless able to renounce their vows of celibacy at any time and return to their former lives. While the rest of society may regret this lost opportunity to progress towards Enlightenment, monks who decide to take this course are not ostracized. The worst sin would be to break one's vows by committing actions that are forbidden to a monk. Monks generally live in monasteries, where they are allotted tasks according to their intellectual, artistic or sometimes even administrative capabilities. Some pursue lengthy studies in philosophy, and after periods of meditation and

'Buddhist compassion has nothing to do with emotion. It is completely objective, cold, and linked to a metaphysical concept. It is not spontaneous, but the consequence of prolonged meditation.'
Jacques Bacot

The words of the Tibetan scholar Jacques Bacot are reflected by the man meditating in his cave (opposite, above). But compassion can also be attained through rituals, as practised by monks, nuns (opposite, below), and this tantrist (left), who is wearing bone ornaments.

learning from the teachings of masters, become lamas themselves.

A lama is a spiritual teacher, but not necessarily a monk; that is to say, he has not taken certain vows, in particular those of celibacy. If he is a monk, he wears a monk's robes, or a form of dress somewhere in between that of a monk and a lay person, and he does not shave his head. Among the Nyingmapa and the Bönpo, in particular, many lamas wear their hair long, tied back in either a bun or a braid. Other holy men, married or unmarried and frequently specializing in rites of exorcism, are known as *nagpa*, or 'tantrists'. Finally, ascetics (*drubthob* or *gomchen*) elect to live as hermits, devoting their lives to solitary meditation.

Nuns (*ani*) are less numerous than monks. The number of vows they take varies slightly between the different schools, but at around 360 is substantially higher than the 250 required of monks. At the same time, there is no tradition of fully ordained nuns in Tibet, and full ordination has only been possible since 1982. Living for the most part in separate monasteries from monks, nuns are nevertheless placed under the authority of a male spiritual teacher. There are also some women – usually the wives of spiritual teachers – who share the religious vocation but are not nuns.

Lines of reincarnation, the *tulku*

Religious life in Tibet is characterized by a great deal of flexibility between its different categories, and nothing prevents people from moving from one category to another, according to their aspirations. However, there is one religious class into which it is impossible to progress,

Incarnate lamas, or *tulku*, are unique to Tibetan Buddhism. At an early age they are recognized as reincarnations of their predecessors, then installed, and given the best possible education. Their aura reflects the prestige of their lineage, but they are always highly respected. In 1992, at the age of seven, the 17th Karmapa, Urgyen Trinley Dorje, arrived amid great ceremony at Tsurphu Monastery in central Tibet (above) from his home in Kham. Despite a show of Chinese 'benevolence', he fled to India in January 2000.

which is that of the incarnate lamas, who are known as the *tulku*, or 'emanated bodies', and who are addressed as *rinpoche*, or 'Precious One' – an honorary title also given to great religious figures who are not *tulku*. The state of reincarnation is one of the distinctive features of Tibetan Buddhism – a condition that Western society would equate with genetics; it is an integral and inalienable part of a child from birth. The child inherits the spiritual heritage which belonged to his predecessor in the line. He is therefore both himself and his predecessors at the same time, and so he bears the same name as them. A lineage of reincarnations begins when a guru declares that he will be born again in this world for the good of others.

Theologically justified by the theory of the Three Bodies of the Buddha, who can take on the form of an 'emanated body' (*tulku*) in our world, there is not in fact any historical mention of these incarnate lineages until the 13th century, when the Karmapa school was the first to introduce them. This form of succession for the hierarchs at the head of religious orders or monasteries gradually supplanted that of family succession, except among the

Once a *tulku* has been found by the entourage of his predecessor, he has to pass various selection tests, and finally must be recognized by a great lama. Nowadays it is usually the Dalai Lama who authenticates the child. Below, the Dalai Lama is placing a sash of benediction on the young Kalu Rinpoche, of the Kagyupa school. His predecessor, Kalu Rinpoche (1905–89), was a gifted teacher who helped to spread Tibetan Buddhism to the West.

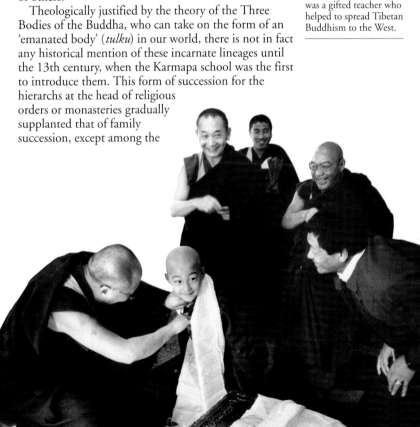

Drukpa Kagyupa until the beginning of the 17th century, and the leaders of the Sakyapa school right up until the present day. Sometimes it even happened that the two methods coincided, and the reincarnated child proved also to be related to his predecessor.

When an incarnate lama dies, he is not regarded as dead but as 'absent'. When the child in whom he is reincarnated has been recognized, he is said to have returned. Recognition takes place after a complex process of prophecies, natural and supernatural signs, divinations, and a study of objects that had belonged to the previous incarnation. Sometimes there are several candidates, which can lead to religious and political problems. The child must ultimately be recognized formally by another great incarnate lama – often the Dalai Lama himself, now in exile – whereas in Chinese Tibet, it is the Chinese government that has now allocated this task to itself. Once the child has been recognized as the incarnation of his predecessor in the line, he is enthroned and takes the name of the lineage. Some of these *tulku* are also great spiritual teachers, or lamas, but except in the Gelugpa school, they are not obliged to take the vow of celibacy.

The pantheon

Whatever the religious school, Bönpo as well as Buddhist, the Tibetan pantheon contains an extraordinary and sometimes surprising profusion of deities of all kinds. These deities are personifications of philosophical symbols, and have no reality of

their own. The organization of this pantheon is complicated, and the deities take on different forms according to what aspects they are meant to symbolize. For ordinary Tibetans, however, they exist and can be approached by means of various rituals. Those deities that do not belong to the Buddhist religion but have been 'converted' into protectors of Buddhism are at the foot of the divine hierarchy, but they are still very important in daily life, because a family's prosperity may depend on them, in the form of good health, the harvest, and the cattle. The names and representations of these deities vary somewhat according to the different schools. They may be divided schematically into those of the

The bodhisattva of compassion, Avalokiteshvara, has several forms, one with eleven heads (opposite, 7th century). At the top of the hierarchy of deities are those that represent esoteric teachings. Above, the *Kalachakra*, the Wheel of Time, situated at the centre of a mandala. This diagram allows the initiated to become one with the divine.

The deities of esoteric cycles are complex and are often shown in sexual union with their consorts, symbolizing the union between compassion and wisdom which will eventually lead to Enlightenment. Opposite, Hevajra, deity of the tantra of the same name, and his consort, Nairatma, trampling the four illusions (Mara) underfoot (15th–16th century). The many hands carry attributes symbolizing their power. The necklaces of heads and the beings trampled underfoot are spirits or harmful desires that have been vanquished.

Iconographically and symbolically, the exact opposite of these tutelary deities is Tara (left, 16th century). Born from the tears shed by Avalokiteshvara out of pity for human beings, Tara is the female counterpart of this bodhisattva of compassion, and like him, she carries the attribute of the lotus, which stands for purity. She is an extremely popular deity, particularly among women. There are twenty-one forms of Tara, of which the best known are White Tara and Green Tara.

great tantric cycles, primordial Buddhas that may be peaceful or savage, Enlightened beings who are in the process of 'becoming Buddhas' (bodhisattvas), and also local deities.

Rituals and practices

Rituals (Tibetan: *choga, rimgro, to*; Sanskrit: *puja*) are a dominant feature of religious practice, and the Tibetans divide these into four categories: appeasement, development, submission, and destruction. Within this scheme, aims may range from pacifying or even exorcizing angry spirits to achieving long life, a safe journey, the prosperity of a region or country, a good harvest. There are also funeral rites and ceremonies commemorating important religious events.

The form that the ceremony takes will therefore depend on its type, its aim, the deity to which it is dedicated, and the religious school performing it. These rituals are often complex, and require elaborate preparations, such as ritual cakes (*torma*) and special offerings, a liturgy of song and recitation, different

The most popular daily practice is *sang*, or incense burning, a ritual of pre-Buddhist origin which pleases local deities and has a purifying effect. Prostration is also important as a mark of faith and of respect. The square in front of Jokhang Temple in Lhasa is the most sacred site for these activities (above). In the morning, bathed in fragrant smoke, hundreds of worshippers prostrate themselves full length, accumulating merits for their future life. At this altitude, physical exertion is a form of asceticism, especially when it is repeated dozens of times.

musical instruments and sometimes different music for the various parts of the same ceremony. They may be addressed to the Buddha, to Padmasambhava, to the deities of the pantheon, or to local gods. Those who perform the rituals will usually be members of the clergy, though not necessarily monks, or may simply be the head of a family if it is a matter of daily worship. Ceremonies may take place in a temple, a private chapel, or even a holy site in the open air if the deities addressed are not Buddhist.

The religious practices and fervour of the Tibetans are intense, and they are manifested daily in simple acts such as offerings of incense, butter lamps and bowls of water (symbolizing the senses), prayers, and circumambulation of holy sites. They are also manifested in local events: putting up prayer flags, pilgrimages, worship of relics, giving religious objects to the temples, participation in collective instruction, and building chortens. The aim of these practices, as far as lay people are concerned, is not so much to attain Enlightenment

Whether a ritual has been requested by a particular family, or takes place as a celebration inside a temple, every one requires physical and spiritual preparation. In addition to the recitation or singing of particular texts, each ceremony has its own liturgy and music. The singing master conducts the songs and holds the cymbals, while other musicians play instruments, including the oboe (left). Among the ritual objects used are the *dorje* (Tibetan) or *vajra* (Sanskrit), meaning 'thunderbolt' (above), and the bell, symbolizing compassion and wisdom. Also important are sacrificial cakes made from grain.

as to accumulate merit, with a view to gaining a better incarnation in the next life that might take them closer to Enlightenment. It is generally believed that only holy men can hope for Enlightenment in this life, and even then, only those who have been given intensive tantric instruction.

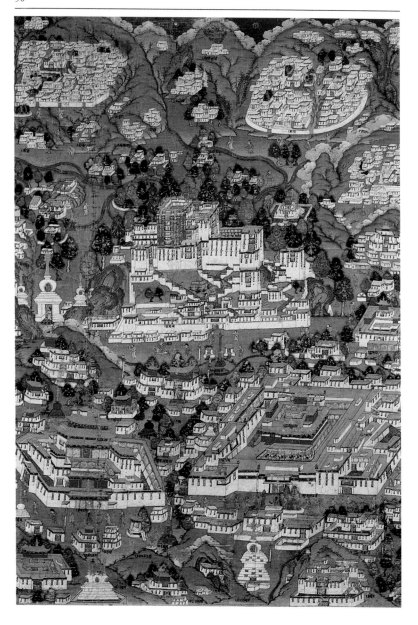

'When you gallop on horseback across the plateau… do you not feel your heart swell with courage? According to the annals of the Tang, our ancestors… wore hats decorated with feathers and horns, and when they galloped away, they cried "Kihaha!" just as we do today,' exclaimed the poet Gedun Chöphel in 1950. While this enthusiasm enabled the Tibetans to build an empire, their conversion to Buddhism led to a symbiosis between state and religion that was to dominate the political scene until 1959.

CHAPTER 3

KINGS AND LAMAS: FROM EMPIRE TO THEOCRACY

The monuments of Lhasa, the Potala, the Jokhang and its monasteries are all illustrated in this 19th-century painting which is a condensed version of Tibetan history (left). It also features Samye Monastery, built by King Trisong Detsen (755–97?) (right, 15th-century statue in Gyantse).

An empire emerges from the high plateaux

Tibet arrived on the historical scene in the 7th century AD, and within a hundred years it ruled over a vast territory extending from north of the borders of Central Asia as far as China. Traces of settlements, in the form of stone tools, actually go back to the Paleolithic era, and remains of Neolithic settlements – cave paintings and carvings, pottery, burial sites – have been found all over the region. The 'Metal Age' covers a long period (from the 2nd millennium to the 6th century AD), and has left behind megaliths, tombs, and metal objects featuring animal motifs akin to the art of the steppes, though a lack of archaeological

information makes them difficult to pinpoint. As for the social and political organization of the inhabitants during this early history, it is still unknown.

The chronology of the pre-monarchic period is equally vague. It might have been in the 6th century, or between the 2nd and 6th centuries, for Tibetan tradition speaks of a series of kings beginning in the 2nd or 3rd century, which would have been the Pugyal dynasty.

Society was probably divided into clans, ruled by

King Songtsen Gampo (above, portrait in the Potala) built the Tibetan empire in the 7th century through a series of rapid conquests. The story of this king, who was considered to be an incarnation of Avalokiteshvara, was retrospectively given a marked Buddhist slant by a text-treasure 'discovered' in the 12th century. 'Treasures' (*terma*) are texts or sacred objects said to have been concealed by Padmasambhava or his disciples so that they might be discovered at the right moment by a predestined master, the 'treasure finder' (*terton*).

independent lords and linked together by marriage. From that time onwards, Chinese annals recorded all information about Tibet as *Tufan*, and today they refer to the pre-monarchic and monarchic periods as *Tubo* or *Tufan*.

At the end of the 6th century, Namri Songtsen, one of the chiefs of the fertile valley of the Yarlung – a tributary of the Tsangpo (Brahmaputra) south-east of present-day Lhasa – began a campaign to unify the principalities of Central Tibet. His son Songtsen Gampo (*c.* 620–49) consolidated his father's achievements, set up his main residence in Lhasa, and from 640 made a series of bold, if not lasting, conquests: the valley of Kathmandu, west of Tibet, the annexation of Zhang Zhung which also encompassed western Nepal, south-eastern Tibet, and even the regions surrounding Lake Kokonor, which were inhabited by several different groups of Turco-Mongols. The king was required to take several wives, including a Nepalese princess and a Chinese princess, as a sign of these mighty political alliances.

Arising from the heart of Asia, the Tibetan empire spread and even took over the far western regions of Sichuan in Tang China. In 703 the Tibetan armies invaded Jan (part of what was to become Nanzhao) to the north-west of Yunnan, the land of horses and salt.

Advancing on China and Central Asia

For more than a century Tibet spread terror with its travelling armies, and carved out a place for itself on the map of Asia. This expansion brought Tibetans and Chinese head to head in a struggle for dominance over China's frontier lands, which included the oases of Central Asia and the turbulent region of Yunnan. Every year there was an exchange of tributes between these great neighbours – the

In order to consolidate his political alliances, King Songtsen Gampo married women from different countries. The most famous were Bhrikuti, a Nepalese princess (opposite below) and Wencheng, a Chinese princess (below; statues in the Potala). The founding of the temples of Jokhang and Ramoche are attributed respectively to these two princesses, and they are considered to have been emanations of Green Tara and White Tara.

kings of Kathmandu, the Palas of Bengal, and the Tang Dynasty.

The most significant expansion of the Tibetan empire took place in the 8th century, under a descendant of Songtsen Gampo, King Trisong Detsen (*c.* 755–97). He took advantage of a Tang empire weakened by the revolt of the Turco-Sogdian governor An Lushan and also by attacks from Arab-Turkish forces. The latter began their expansion into the Tarim oases after their victory over the Chinese in the Battle of Talas (now Kyrgyzstan) in 751. During the same period the Tibetans became allies of the kingdom of Nanzhao in Yunnan, and in 763, backed up by Uighur forces, they penetrated as far as the Chinese capital Chang'an (Xian), which they sacked before abandoning it. Peace was finally signed with China in 783, by which time the Tibetans controlled the oases of Central Asia, including Dunhuang. In 790 they reached the Amudarya river and the horse-rich region of Ferghana, which marked the furthest point of their

This modern map shows cultural and ethnic Tibet in the 7th and 8th centuries. The source material from this period includes the Dunhuang manuscripts which, despite their fragmentary state, are of incalculable historical and religious interest. The oasis of Dunhuang (opposite, a 9th-century drawing of the site) was strategically situated on the Silk Road, and was occupied during the 8th and 9th centuries by the Tibetans, who therefore came into contact with other Central Asian peoples.

expansion to the west, since they were held back by the forces of Harun al-Rashid, caliph of Baghdad.

A colossus with feet of clay...

The death of Trisong Detsen at the end of the 8th century sowed the seeds of the empire's disintegration. The Arabs formed an alliance with the Chinese, while the Uighurs – who were now at the height of their expansionist powers – continually harassed the oasis garrisons of the Tibetans in Central Asia. There were further futile skirmishes with China in the north-west until a new peace treaty was signed in 822–23. The text, which fixed the borders of the two empires, was written

Written in Chinese, Tibetan, Sanskrit and Uighur, the Dunhuang manuscripts were discovered *c.* 1900 – hidden in the walls of a cave in the oasis – by Wang, a Chinese Taoist monk. The scholars Aurel Stein in 1907, and Paul Pelliot in 1908, on archaeological expeditions to Central Asia, heard of this discovery, visited the cave, and both bought

in Chinese and Tibetan on three stone pillars: one in Chang'an, the second on the Tibetan-Chinese border, and the third in Lhasa. In 842 the Tibetan dynasty collapsed with the murder of King Lang Darma, which later Buddhist histories interpret as anti-Buddhist, though recently discovered documents suggest that this point of view may require some revision.

The fall of the Tibetan dynasty and the annihilation of the Uighur state by its old enemies from Kyrgyzstan,

a large number of the manuscripts from Wang. These have since been kept in the British Museum in London and the Bibliothèque Nationale in Paris, and are slowly being published. Microfilm copies have also been given to China.

resulted in further destabilization of this area of Central Asia. The Chinese renewed old alliances, and the Tibetans were driven out of the oases, including Dunhuang, Khotan and Hami. Tang China was, for the moment, the winner of the ultimate prize – control of the trade routes between China and Persia, and domination of the 'Barbarians from the West'.

By the sheer scale of its conquests, which brought with them a variety of peoples who could not be controlled, the Tibetan empire had proved to be a colossus with feet of clay. In fact ever since the time of King Songtsen Gampo, the various political marriages and changing regional alliances had been linked to a chain of brilliant conquests and swift losses, with the decline of the dynasty being exacerbated by religious conflict between Buddhism and the religion that had preceded it. It was a period of palace intrigues which involved a succession of plots and assassinations.

...but a cultural boom

Despite all of this, the dynastic era was also marked by a remarkable cultural and intellectual development. The Tibetans were influenced not only by the Chinese and Indian civilizations, but also by those of Zhang Zhung in western Tibet and the Greeks and Iranians. By merging these with their own indigenous traditions, they created the foundations of Tibetan culture as it is known today. They established a written language still in use, they translated canonical texts from Sanskrit into Tibetan, and Buddhism became the official state religion in the 8th century.

In the Tibetan view, 'three kings according to Buddhist law' (*chögyel sum*) played a major role: Songtsen Gampo, who is credited with the introduction of Buddhism, but who in fact maintained strong links with the pre-Buddhist religion; Trisong Detsen (755–97?), who built Samye, the first monastery, in 775 with the help of the Indian mystic Padmasambhava, and made Buddhism the state religion in 779; and Relpachen (815–38), along with his father, Senaleg (804?–15). The two latter kings

During the building of Samye Monastery, local deities were impeding the work. Trisong Detsen asked Padmasambhava to subjugate them, but when the two met, the king refused to bow to the guru who, with a gesture of authority, produced a jet of flame from his fingers... and the king prostrated himself (19th-century painting, Samye).

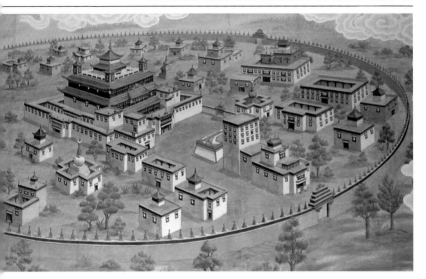

invited several spiritual teachers from India and Nepal – one result being a Buddhist Sanskrit-Tibetan dictionary still in use today, the *Mahavyutpatti* – and gave certain privileges to the clergy and the monasteries. This promotion of Buddhism annoyed the followers of the pre-Buddhist religion, who were present in large numbers in the court itself, and may have been at the root of Relpachen's assassination in 838 at the hands of his brother, Lang Darma, who was later depicted as a persecutor of the Buddhists. Lang Darma was in turn assassinated by a Buddhist monk in 842, and in little more than a hundred years, Tibet disappeared from the world stage.

After a century of obscurity, a Buddhist revival

Between 852 and 970 it is difficult to know what happened in Tibet, since no contemporary documents survive – not

Samye Monastery (modern painting, Tsetang) was built on the plan of the Odantapuri temple in India. It is a three-dimensional cosmic mandala, with the central tower representing the axis of the world – Mount Sumeru (or Meru) – the outbuildings being the continents, and the perimeter of chortens the wall of iron. The monastery was badly damaged during the Cultural Revolution, but has recently been restored; this stone pillar, dating from the 8th century (left), miraculously survived. The inscribed edict established Buddhism as the state religion.

Tibetan monasteries were laid out in two different ways. The older ones, such as Samye (left, 19th-century painting) and Tholing (see overleaf) were built on flat terrain and often followed the mandala plan of Indian monasteries. From the 11th century onwards, however, they were constructed like fortified towns, with the buildings huddling below sheltered places on mountainsides, or even standing like true fortresses on rocky slopes. Whatever their layout, the buildings always served the same purposes: temples of different sizes, some with courtyards, a shrine to protective deities, cells or little houses for the monks, a kitchen, different storerooms, and toilets. Books were kept in the temples where teaching also took place, although some students went to the masters' homes. The monasteries were built of natural stone and wood which was sometimes transported over hundreds of miles. All the woodwork was first assembled on the ground (left).

even in Chinese. Buddhism was uprooted by the loss of its monastic communities and its royal patronage, but did survive in isolated pockets. The Buddhist revival sprang both from Amdo, in the east of Tibet, where some monks had taken refuge, and from the west, due to descendants of the scattered royal family who had established their own kingdom of Guge. It covered what was once Zhang Zhung, and was made up of the regions of Guge, Purang, Ladakh, Spiti and Kinnaur.

At the end of the 10th century, in order to re-establish Buddhism, the kings of western Tibet sent some young people to Kashmir and India, where they became translators. The most famous of these was Rinchen Zangpo (958–1055), who translated canonical texts, and revised the ancient tantras; he is credited with founding temples throughout the whole of western Tibet. Yeshe Ö, a Buddhist king of Guge, sponsored the building of monasteries – Tholing and Tabo – in 996. In 1042 his descendant Changchup Ö invited Atisha, a Bengali pandit and great Buddhist scholar, to take part in the Tibetan Buddhist renaissance. Atisha inspired a real revival both of the doctrines and of monastic life in Tibet, until his death in 1056. His disciples called themselves Kadampa – 'those who follow oral teachings'.

In the 10th and 11th centuries, western Tibet was a centre for the renaissance of Buddhism, and its proximity to India allowed the Tibetans to receive teachings from Indian masters. These included Rinchen Zangpo (above, painting from Alchi, Ladakh, c. 1200), who played a vital role in translating and disseminating Buddhist texts as well as the cult of the supreme Buddha; also Vairochana (below, painting from Tsaparang, 16th century), who is the principal figure in the tantra of that name. This text was immensely popular, in Japan too, as it brought together several other tantras.

The second diffusion of Buddhism: when faith met politics

During this time, monks who had taken monastic vows returned from eastern to Central Tibet, and set about establishing small communities. The whole land was a hive of spiritual and intellectual fervour. Many Tibetans went off to India, Nepal and Kashmir to seek out instruction, and this movement only ended with the Muslim invasions at the beginning of the 13th century.

This second wave of Buddhism is significant from both a spiritual and a political point of view. Given the importance of both teachers and oral teachings in tantric Buddhism, several charismatic figures emerged who gathered many disciples around them. These communities were supported by lay 'patron-donors', who helped them to build monasteries. Little by little, these monasteries grew to be centres of theology and literature, but also of economic power, thanks to gifts of land and cattle. Every school built monasteries affiliated to their main centre, and all tried to extend their religious influence as far as possible. Because of their prestige and the veneration in which they were held, monks began to play a larger role in negotiations between local lords.

In prehistoric times, western Tibet (Ngari) was the cradle of Zhang Zhung culture – of which hardly any trace now remains – and of the Bön religion; in the 10th century it was at the heart of the Buddhist renaissance, and until the 17th century it was the centre of the Guge kingdom, one of whose capitals was Tholing (below), situated in the magnificent Sutlej Canyon. Tholing was one of the first Tibetan monasteries (996) and like Samye, was built on a mandala plan. Despite the fact that it was a long way away from any centres of power, it was very badly damaged during the Cultural Revolution.

Unobtrusively, then, the Buddhist schools – already powerful forces in matters of religion and economics – became increasingly active politically, filling the power vacuum that had been left by the fall of the monarchy.

The Sakyapa and the Mongols

From the 13th to the beginning of the 17th century, the religious schools vied for political power, sometimes not directly in their own name, but through their alliances with powerful patron-donors, some of whom were not even Tibetan. The first school actually to assume political power, between 1260 and 1354, was that of the Sakyapa, who entered into a relationship of patronage with the Mongols. The armies of the latter launched many destructive raids against Central Tibet, but they received religious instruction from the lamas, spared Tibet, and actually became its protectors. Kublai Khan gave religious and political jurisdiction over the whole of Tibet to Phagpa, a Sakyapa lama, and when he became Emperor of China in 1260, the prestige of the Sakyapa grew still further. Succession from uncle to nephew within these religious schools ensured that the Sakya family held on to the reins of power. The influence of the Mongols was also a key factor in the complete reorganization of the Tibetan administrative system, titles, ranks, and costumes.

In the second half of the 14th century, the Sakyapa lost power to the Phagmodrupa, a branch of the Kagyupa whose most famous representative was Changchup Gyaltsen (1302–73), who severed all contact with the Mongol Yuan dynasty, and then with that of the Chinese Ming dynasty which succeeded it. He gained independence for Tibet, and established the administrative system of the *dzong* – or 'fortress-districts'.

The lama Sakya Pandita(1182–1251; 15th-century statue below), regarded as Tibet's greatest sage, was head of the Sakyapa school. In 1244 he was summoned to the region of Kokonor, where the Mongol prince Goden had set up camp and wished to receive instruction. Sakya Pandita remained at the prince's court until he died, and contributed greatly to the status of the Sakyapa from both a religious and a political point of view, because this was the beginning of their ascendancy in Central Tibet.

The Karmapa and the Gelugpa – rivals in the 15th and 16th centuries

Meanwhile, a new factor had emerged in Central Tibet, which was to transform the political and religious landscape. Tsongkhapa (1357–1419), a master from Amdo who had come to Central Tibet, attracted a number of disciples and lay patrons with his teachings. He preached a strict, reformed version of Buddhism, and his school took the name of Gelugpa, 'the Virtuous'. It revived the traditional teachings of the Kadampa, and was so successful that several large Gelugpa monasteries were founded in the Lhasa region, at Drepung, Sera and Ganden.

From the 12th century, first the Karmapa and then the Gelugpa broke with the system of hereditary power, and

Phagpa (1235–80), nephew of Sakya Pandita, accompanied his uncle to Kokonor. He was the first to enter into a formal relationship of patronage with a foreign leader, in this case the king of the Mongols, Kublai Khan (1215–94). The two men are shown in the painting above (Gyantse, 15th century), seated on a level with one another, to represent the equality of their relationship.

organized succession to the leadership of their school through lines of descent by reincarnation, the *tulku*. This system, which was later adopted by the other schools, brought about a profound political and religious change

The Kagyupa school split into several branches, of which today only the Drungpa, the Drukpa and the

in Tibet. In 1407, the 4th head of the Karmapa school and, some years later, the nephew of Tsongkhapa went to Beijing at the invitation of the Ming dynasty, but links between Tibetan Buddhism and China were not as close as they were during the Yuan period.

In 1434 the Phagmodrupa, who still had a degree of political control over Tibet, were challenged by the chiefs of Rinpung, an area north of Shigatse. There followed two centuries of sometimes insidious and sometimes open hostility between the two most important religious schools in Central Tibet at that time – the Karmapa and the Gelugpa – often brought about by the lay protectors to whom their fate was bound. The Karmapa were supported by the lords of Rinpung, while the Gelugpa were under the protection of the Phagmodrupa chiefs of the Lhasa region. The overthrow of the lords of Rinpung by one of their own feudal lords made no difference, as he installed himself at Shigatse, assuming the title 'King

Karmapa have survived. In the 15th and 16th centuries the Karmapa became rivals of the Gelugpa, who had established their main monasteries – including Drepung (above) – near Lhasa. Central Tibet was a battleground between these two schools until the Gelugpa emerged victorious in the early 17th century.

of Tsang', and his descendants continued to support the Karmapa. The Gelugpa found themselves in a difficult situation, because the Phagmodrupa were getting weaker and weaker.

The Mongols support the Gelugpa

In 1577 Sonam Gyatso, the 3rd Abbot of Drepung, was invited to Mongolia by Altan Khan, chief of the Mongol tribe of Tumed. He arrived there in 1578, and that is a highly significant date in the history of Tibet, for it marks the conversion of Altan Khan and his people to the Gelugpa school of Buddhism, as well as the conferment upon Sonam Gyatso of the Mongol title Dalai Lama. The Mongols became fervent and ferocious supporters of the Gelugpa, and the title of Dalai Lama was conferred

Scholarly debate (below) demanded knowledge of the texts, advanced logic, and great presence of mind. Noisily conducted by groups of monks, it took place in a monastery courtyard, sheltered from the wind. The questioner stood upright, facing his interlocutor, who was seated. Mime and gesture were important factors because he had to unsettle his adversary, and questions were not the only permitted means of doing so. The sound of prayer beads, hand claps, the thud of boots on the ground – these could all be used to break an opponent's concentration. This verbal jousting did not exist in the Kagyupa or Nyingmapa schools.

retrospectively on Sonam Gyatso's two predecessors on the throne of Drepung. After Sonam Gyatso's death in 1588, on his way back to Tibet, the 4th Dalai Lama (1589–1617) was chosen from among Altan Khan's close relations.

Although they now had the support of the Mongols, the Gelugpa were hardly in a position of any power in Central Tibet. It only needed the flimsiest of pretexts for hostilities to be resumed: an exchange of insults, failure to show respect, destruction of property. In 1605 the King of Tsang and the Karmapa drove the Mongols out of the region of Lhasa, and for years tensions remained high, culminating in attacks on Gelugpa monasteries by Tsang troops in 1618.

Amid this political and religious turmoil, the recognition of the 5th Dalai Lama remained a closely guarded secret, because the Gelugpa feared for his life. Finally, after the Mongols attacked Tsang forces not far from Lhasa, the situation eased a little, and in 1622 the 5th Dalai Lama was publicly revealed and the child was enthroned at Drepung Monastery.

The rise of the Dalai Lamas, and 'The Great Fifth' (1617–82)

The 5th Dalai Lama is known by the Tibetans as 'The Great Fifth', because he gave Tibet a greatness and influence unequalled since the days of the empire. The incarnation of the bodhisattva Avalokiteshvara and of King Songtsen Gampo, it was he who consolidated the temporal supremacy of the line of Dalai Lamas and the Gelugpa school in Tibet. Linking back across the centuries to the imperial tradition, he moved his residence to the Potala in Lhasa, and made the city into a renowned capital. A scholar and a mystic, a remarkable politician, and a fine writer, he became one of the leading figures in Tibetan history.

In order to establish his power and to get rid of his enemies, the young Dalai Lama turned to the Mongol allies of the Gelugpa, and in particular to Gushri Khan, of the

In Samye Monastery is a large 19th-century panel depicting donors from the different regions to which the influence of Tibetan Buddhism had spread (above). The Mongols and the Manchus are recognizable by their hats, while the people of the southern Himalayas wear turbans and elephant tusks; they are all keen to present their offerings to the 5th Dalai Lama and to receive his blessing (opposite). Two monks, at the foot of his throne, are trying to get them in line and re-establish ceremonial order.

Qoshot tribe. The latter launched his army first against eastern Tibet, and then against central Tibet, where he defeated the King of Tsang and the Karmapa. In 1642 a great ceremony was held in Shigatse, capital of Tsang, where the 5th Dalai Lama was invested by Gushri Khan with temporal power over the whole of Tibet, thus re-establishing the relationship of patronage that had begun in the 13th century with the Sakyapa lama Phagpa and Kublai Khan. The Manchu Qing dynasty thought that the 5th Dalai Lama would be able to control the wild Mongols, and invited him to Beijing in 1652–53.

The period from 1670 to 1685 was one of conquest: the Chumbi valley in the south of Tibet, some regions of Kham, and the western area of Tibet that had been under the control of Ladakh; only Bhutan succeeded in resisting this advance. These territorial conquests, which reunited Tibet for the first time since the empire, were naturally accompanied by the building of great Gelugpa monasteries. After the death in 1662 of his tutor, the

The greatest protector of the 5th Dalai Lama was the Mongol chief Gushri Khan (1582–1655; opposite below), who in 1642 masterminded the military and political victory of the 5th Dalai Lama's Gelugpa supporters over the King of Tsang, who supported the Karmapa. The 'Great Fifth', born into a noble family near Samye, was learned, pious and humorous. His political instinct made him leave Drepung Monastery and establish Lhasa as the political centre of Tibet, with the Potala Palace as his symbol.

Panchen Lama, the Dalai Lama introduced descent by reincarnation for the Panchen Lamas, who resided in Tashilunpo, near Shigatse. These two lines, however, were later to come into frequent political conflict.

This temporal power, gained with the support of the Mongol Qoshot tribe, was to have political consequences following the death in 1682 of the great statesman, whose life began and ended with a secret. Just as his accession had been kept hidden, his death was concealed by his regent, the *desi* (regent) Sangye Gyatso (1653–1705), a scholar of medicine and a statesman who, in order not to destabilize the political situation, preferred

not to announce the news. It was not made public until 1696, to the fury of the Qing dynasty, whose emissaries had been fobbed off in 1690, and the Mongols, who accused the regent of trying to keep power for himself.

Tashilunpo, the monastery of the Panchen Lamas, near Shigatse (drawing by Sven Hedin, 1907).

The latter was assassinated by Lhazang Khan, chief of the Qoshot, in 1705.

The 6th Dalai Lama ascended the throne at the age of 13. For a Gelugpa master, he was an eccentric character, and although his refusal to take all the monastic vows and his love of poetry and women endeared him to the people, it infuriated the Mongols and the Qing, who had already begun to lose confidence in the Tibetan regime.

The influence of the Qing dynasty – an 18th-century power struggle

The power vacuum, the absence of a strong and respected leader, and the turbulence of the Mongols all contributed to thirty years of trouble for Tibet, increasingly from the Qing. The 6th Dalai Lama was deposed, and died on his way into exile. Two Mongol groups took it in turn to occupy Central Tibet: the Qoshot, supported by the Qing Emperor Kangxi, and then the Dzungar in 1717; at first these were welcomed as liberators, but then they plundered and destroyed the monasteries that were not Gelugpa. The 7th Dalai Lama (1708–57), Kelsang Gyatso, who was born in Kham, was hidden from the Dzungar by his father and took refuge at Kumbum Monastery in Amdo, in north-eastern Tibet, where he was 'protected' by the Qing dynasty. The child was a political pawn, and in 1720 he was taken to Lhasa by a Manchu army which joined forces with the Tibetan troops under two generals and drove away the Dzungar. The Tibetans were therefore indebted to the Qing but did not realize the extent to which the country had now been placed under Qing influence.

The pro and anti-Qing struggle at the heart of collegial power intensified in Lhasa. The 7th Dalai Lama and his family were anti-Qing. The violent seizure of power by General Phola marked the beginnings of direct Chinese influence on the conduct of Tibetan affairs. The 7th Dalai Lama was banished to the extreme west of the country, parts of eastern Kham and Amdo passed into

Out of veneration for his master Lobsang Chögyen (1569–1662; opposite above, 18th-century painting) the 5th Dalai Lama established a lineage for the Panchen Lamas, who were considered to be the incarnation of the Buddha Amitabha (above, late 15th-century painting). Amithaba was the tutelary Buddha to Avalokiteshvara, of whom the Dalai Lamas are emanations. Lobsang Chögyen, who lived at Tashilunpo Monastery, was the first Panchen Lama, but the title was given retrospectively to his predecessors, and it was decreed that Kedrup Je (1385–1438) one of Tsongkhapa's disciples, was the first of the line. Tashilunpo Monastery, built in 1447, became the seat of this lineage during the 17th century.

the hands of the Qing, and small Chinese garrisons were set up in several regions, while two imperial Manchu commissioners, the *amban*, were posted to Lhasa and Shigatse. Titles and honours were granted to Tibetan nobles, and there was a huge increase in trade. The 'reign' of Phola (1728–47) was important because this was the first lay government that Tibet had had since the days of its empire. Phola, a statesman and diplomat, was able to stabilize the country, as the Manchus trusted him, and he succeeded in confining their interference in Tibetan affairs to a purely formal level.

When he died, power passed between the hands of the regents, Gelugpa followers, and for more than a century Tibetan politics took the form of intrigues among powerful ministers and the great families. Dalai Lamas succeeded one another without really assuming power, especially since the 8th had little interest in temporal affairs, and the 9th to the 12th all died young. The Panchen Lamas turned to the Qing. Because of quarrels over the minting of coins, the Tibetans were frequently attacked by Gurkha forces from Nepal, and needed the help of Manchu troops to repel them. As for the Manchus themselves, they were anxious to prevent the Tibetans from falling into the hands of the British or Russians, and so they supported the decision at the beginning of the 19th century to close Tibet to the West.

If Tibet was very much under the influence of the Manchus during the 18th century, this became weaker throughout the 19th century, the Qing dynasty having other more pressing priorities. Their garrisons were reduced to merely providing escorts, the *amban* regarded their posts as an exile, and relations between the Tibetans and the Manchus dwindled to an exchange of gifts and courtesies.

From the end of the 18th century relations between Tibet and Nepal deteriorated, giving rise to several armed expeditions. The Himalayas were not an impassable barrier, and the trade route through Kyirong also became an invasion route for the Gurkha army of Nepal, as happened in 1855 (below). On the pretext

of trade violations by the Tibetans, the Gurkhas – led by the powerful minister Jung Bahadur Rana – occupied the frontier districts of southern Tibet; this invasion brought them into conflict with the Tibetan troops. A complex treaty of 1856 redefined relations between the two countries.

The 13th Dalai Lama, independence and the end of a world

The 13th Dalai Lama, Thubten Gyatso (1876–1933), having survived one assassination attempt, proved to be an outstanding politician at a time when the struggle between the great powers of Russia, Britain and China for supremacy in Central Asia was at its height. The British, who wanted to move into Tibet for commercial reasons, were met with a flat refusal by the Tibetan government. At the same time, rumours persisted of Russian influence over the 13th Dalai Lama – not to mention the possibility of an agreement between Russia and China on the subject of Tibet.

In 1904 the British launched a military expedition against Tibet and signed a trade agreement. The Dalai Lama fled to Mongolia. With the *amban* once more gaining authority in Lhasa, and the Tibetan government

The British East India Company saw it as a priority to establish trading relations with Tibet. In 1774 the emissary George Bogle (far left, in white) went to Shigatse and met Palden Yeshe, the 6th Panchen Lama. The meeting is immortalized in this painting (Tilly Kettle, Calcutta, 1775), which mixes the romantic style of the period with realistic details. Bogle got on well with the Tibetans, and even returned from his mission with a Tibetan wife.

incapable of action in the absence of the Dalai Lama, the latter then went to Beijing in 1908, where he met several diplomats, including the French, and reaffirmed Tibet's stance in relation to the Empress Cixi – the Chinese were once again patrons of Tibet, but nothing more.

From 1905 onwards, in the western regions of Tibet already under the Qing, there was a constant series of rebellions. An *amban* and some French missionaries deemed too close to the Chinese were killed. This revolt brought bloody retribution from the Manchu general Zhao Er Feng, 'the Butcher of Kham'. He imposed reforms based on the Chinese model, and created the province of Xikang in eastern Tibet, becoming its governor in 1908.

In 1909 the Dalai Lama returned to Lhasa after five years of exile, and immediately came into open conflict with the amban, Lian Yu, who called in reinforcements of 2,000 men from Sichuan. Parts of Lhasa were ransacked. The Dalai Lama sent emissaries to the great powers, but these were no longer interested in Tibet. He then went back into exile, this time to British India,

Having failed to achieve their commercial ends, and in the spy mania of the 'Great Game' that was poisoning the whole atmosphere of Central Asia, the British sent an expeditionary force to Tibet in 1904 (below, illustration from *Le Petit Journal*, February 1904). Under the command of Colonel Younghusband, it set out to force the Tibetans to establish relations with British India, and so counterbalance any possible Russian influence. After the massacre at Kuru, the British advanced as far as Lhasa, where they were met by some Tibetan officials.

where he was given a friendly welcome. Great Britain launched an official protest to the Qing court concerning its interference in the internal affairs of Tibet. The period between 1907 and 1911 is in fact the only one prior to modern times in which the Chinese used force to try and impose themselves on Central Tibet, and this attempt caused bitter resentment.

After the fall of the Qing dynasty in 1911, the 13th Dalai Lama officially broke off relations with China and announced that its protection was neither necessary nor desirable. The last Chinese soldiers were driven out of Tibet, and in 1912 the Dalai Lama returned to Lhasa. He was the first Dalai Lama after The Great Fifth to assume political power. In 1914 the British signed an agreement with the Tibetans, recognizing them as equals.

The 13th Dalai Lama, Thubten Gyatso (1876–1933) was a skilled politician (above, in exile at Kalimpong, *c.* 1910), who devoted himself to the cause of Tibet, declaring its independence in 1912 after the fall of the Qing dynasty in China.

The Dalai Lama had to reach compromises with a powerful bureaucracy, the 20,000 monks from the great monasteries around Lhasa – some of whom hankered after the kind of sumptuous gifts they had received from the Manchu emperors – and the Panchen Lama, whose lineage had become a kind of state within a state. Misunderstandings led to the 9th Panchen Lama fleeing to China in 1923. Although there were a few Tibetans, like General Tsarong or the intellectual Gedun Chöphel,

who recognized the need for modernization within Tibetan society, the forces of conservatism were too powerful and were too frightened of the potential damaging changes that might arise from contact with foreigners. Reforms of the army and police were suspended, and the British school, which had been opened in Gyantse in 1924, was closed after two years. The Dalai Lama gave way to the critics of modernization – even on a limited scale – and the chance of opening the country up was lost for ever.

The 13th Dalai Lama died in 1933. The Chinese sent a delegation to convey their condolences, and then reopened their mission. In 1936 a small British mission was opened in Lhasa, with the agreement of the Tibetan government, who were happy to welcome another power as a counterbalance to the Chinese – something which the Nepalese and Bhutanese representatives had never been during their two hundred years in Lhasa.

Furthermore, high society in Tibet was very interested in trading with British India, especially in products such as glass, arms and cotton fabrics. Some noblemen's children were sent to fashionable boarding schools in Darjeeling and Kalimpong, and in 1944 a school was

In 1922 – under the influence of the 13th Dalai Lama, some Tibetan officials and the British – Tibet experienced a very tentative form of modernization. The image above strikingly encapsulates the period. Seated are officials wearing brocaded costumes or Western uniforms, and General Tsarong Dazang Dadul (centre) wears a uniform with lanyards and polished boots, although his hairstyle is Tibetan. An ambitious man, who pursued a policy of openness and also modernized the army, he was dismissed from his posts as commander-in-chief and minister in 1925.

The Tsarongs were a powerful family in Central Tibet and along with the Pandatshangs, who came from eastern Tibet, they controlled part of the great caravan trade (below). This trade between India, Tibet and China required substantial capital, and also involved some risk because of bandits and bad weather. The caravans of yaks and mules were accompanied by armed guards. Cotton goods, tools, rifles and fancy goods came from India, and tea and silk from China, while Tibet exported wool, gold, and musk. The route ran from Central Tibet to Kalimpong in East

opened in Lhasa, but was rapidly forced to close owing to monastic opposition.

The 14th Dalai Lama, Tenzin Gyatso, was born in Amdo in 1935 and ceremonially enthroned in Lhasa in 1940. He was much too young to prevent internal politics from once more degenerating into quarrels between the regents. The country went through the Second World War in a state of blissful ignorance, and both the upper classes and the monks continued to live as if the world had not changed in the slightest, and as if the signs of impending disaster had nothing at all to do with the East. In 1947 the British left India, and in 1949 the Communists took power in China. This was to have dramatic consequences for the fate of Tibet.

India, near Bhutan, and was dominated by Mount Jomolhari (7320 m).

'What then is the formidable charm of this strange country, to which those who have once glimpsed it always return? To rediscover its mountains and its people, one must cross the ocean, traverse entire kingdoms, the whole of China... And one arrives in frozen deserts so high that they no longer seem to belong to the Earth... One sees houses like huge castles, all humming with prayers and smelling of rancid butter and incense. This land is Tibet... forbidden to foreigners, isolated from the world, and so close to the sky....'

Jacques Bacot, 1912

CHAPTER 4

THE QUEST OF THE WEST

In the 18th century, explorers painted watercolours (left, Samuel Davis, 1783). At the beginning of the 20th century, photography became the favoured medium. Opposite: Alexandra David-Néel with Khampa warriors (Kanze, 1924).

"For it is in this part of India that the sandy desert lies. Here, in this desert, there live amid the sand great ants, in size somewhat less than dogs, but bigger than foxes.... Those ants make their dwellings under ground, and like the Greek ants, which they very much resemble in shape, throw up sand–heaps as they burrow. Now the sand which they throw up is full of gold. The Indians... go into the desert to collect this sand.... When the Indians reach the place where the gold is, they fill their bags with the sand, and ride away at their best speed: the ants, however, scenting them, as the Persians say, rush forth in pursuit."

Herodotus, *Histories*

Left, a 15th-century woodcut showing ants digging for gold.

At the beginning of the 20th century, this mythical land of which all Westerners dream was nothing but a large blank patch on the map of Asia. Furthermore, influenced by the rivalry between the three great powers of Russia, China and Britain, it was more than ever a forbidden and jealously guarded country. However, this was not always so, and over the centuries there have been many intrepid travellers who have experienced its mysteries. Missionaries, explorers, representatives from British India, spies and adventurers – all in their different ways told tales of a land and a city that was virtually 'inaccessible', where the grandeur of nature gave rise to such mystical exaltation that dream and reality became confused. There is probably no country in the world that has so excited the human imagination, which has spent hundreds of years trying to penetrate its mystery.

Herodotus was the first writer to allude to Tibet when he wrote of an area in the upper regions of the Indus where there were ants that dug for gold. Subsequently all accounts of Tibet mention the prospectors and gold mines, thus nourishing the myth of a mysterious land full of hidden treasure.

The name 'Tibet' first appeared in Western literature in an account written by the Spanish explorer Benjamin de Tudela. He travelled to Central Asia in the 12th century, and reported 'that a few days' walk away from Samarkand extends the province of Tibet, whose forests provide shelter for the beast which produces musk.' His source is probably Arabic literature which, from the 7th century onwards, mentions Tibet (*Tubbat*) in association with musk – the substance produced by a gland in the male musk deer (*Moschus moschiferus*) and used by the Arabs since antiquity for making perfume. In around the 10th century, Arabic literature also includes the earliest references to a city named Lhasa.

The earliest travellers

The first wave of travel to Central Asia took place in the middle of the 13th century. In 1241 Europe was barely recovering from the terrors of the Mongol invasion, which had ended when the Mongols suddenly withdrew on the death of their khan Ogodei. The Pope and King Louis IX of France (later St Louis) decided to send emissaries to the great Khan of Mongolia in order to find out about

The first detailed, though not entirely accurate map of the Orient, commissioned in around 1290 by the Polo brothers while they were still in China. In 1380 the *Catalan Atlas* shows Asia from the Black Sea to the Pacific Ocean in four sections, and pinpoints the major cities of China. But it is on Fra Mauro's map of 1459 that there is the first clear mention of 'Tebet'. Fra Mauro, a Venetian, was influenced by the maps and accounts of the Polo brothers. The map depicts China in

illustrations that are typical of the Middle Ages. North China with the Yellow River is situated at the bottom, while South China with the Yangtse is at the top. Tibet can be seen on the left of the map (left, detail from Fra Mauro's map, 1459). In the 17th century, Johann Grueber's map showed Tibet as the water tower of Asia, a geographical fact confirmed by explorers two hundred years later.

his future intentions. Jean du Plan Carpin, a Franciscan monk, arrived at the court of Khan Kuyuk in 1246. He returned from this mission and wrote *The History of the Mongols*, in which is to be found the first information on Tibet. He tells how 'the Mongol army reached the country of Burithabet, which it conquered by force; they are pagans who have an incredible and rather deplorable custom that if someone's father has paid his natural tribute to death, all the relations gather round to eat him: we were assured that this was so.' The origin of this rumour was the ritual of the sky burial, and for over two centuries travellers would continue to refer to this in their accounts.

In 1253 another emissary from King Louis, Guillaume de Rubrouk, arrived at the court of Khan Mangu. In his account of this journey, he gave a first impression of Tibetan Buddhism, quoting the famous mantra *om mani battam* (in fact: *Om mani padme hum*), and said that he even took part in a religious debate. He spoke of idolatrous monks who believe in the transmigration of the soul and in spirits, and also reported that there were cannibal men, the 'tebet', who drank from the skulls of their relatives.

Marco Polo was also interested in Tibetan customs. He arrived at the court of Kublai Khan in 1275, where he noted the presence of 'sorcerers' and Tibetan priests.

During his journey, he crossed the border regions of Tibet, which he said were inhabited by bands of ferocious bandits, filthy and idolatrous, but with some surprising customs.

For a long time the Franciscan missionary Odoric of Pordenone was considered to have been the first Westerner to reach Lhasa. He left Europe in 1318 and travelled to the kingdom of Riboth. 'In its white city, named Gota, no one dares to spill human blood, and yet

The compliance attributed to Tibetan women fired Marco Polo's imagination, even though he had never visited the country. 'The old women come with these virgins, their daughters or relatives, and present them to passing strangers....' The illustration (below, *The Travels of Marco Polo, c.* 1400) shows horsemen offering a ring to some young girls, and probably echoes the reference to the traveller who in the morning hands over 'a ring or a little trinket'. The many popular accounts of Marco Polo's travels had a major influence on the way in which Westerners imagined the East from the 15th century onwards.

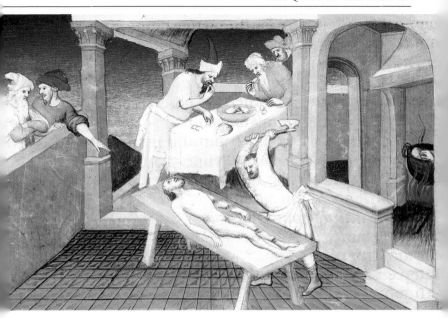

they practise sky burials and other abominable customs.' In fact, Odoric must have gone not to Lhasa but to Khotan, in Central Asia, and was simply repeating information he had been given by the local people.

During the 14th century, the Mongol empire lost its power. It no longer struck fear into the hearts of Europeans, who then stopped sending emissaries. At the same time, new and easier trade routes were opened, and so missionaries and traders ceased to venture forth into the countries of Central Asia. But through the accounts of those who had visited them, these lands remained cloaked in mystery and peopled by phantoms of the medieval imagination.

Missionaries on the roof of the world

At the end of the 16th century, the Society of Jesus, founded in 1534, established missions in India and China which very quickly began to look for lands to convert. Sure enough, they turned their attention to Tibet. Antonio de Andrade, a Portuguese Jesuit, is

The concept of the dismemberment of the dead shocked people from the West. It was described *c.* 1330 by Odoric of Pordenone, who could only have known about it through hearsay; '...they carry the dead body out into the fields, and right there on a table... the priests cut the body into pieces, and then the eagles and vultures come and they throw each one a piece....' (Above, from *The Travels of Marco Polo, c.* 1400; a similar illustration can be found in *The Travels of Sir John Mandeville,* from 1365.)

considered to be the first European to have truly reached the heart of Tibet. He crossed the Himalayas from the west and, although this was an extremely arduous route, he entered the royal city of Tsaparang in 1624, where he was received by the King of Guge. At the time, this independent kingdom was just as important as Central Tibet. In his account, Andrade says how moved he was by the particularly warm welcome he was given by the king, who expressed interest in his religion, and allowed him to set up a mission and build a church. He also found that there were a lot of similarities between the two religions, but deplored the evident hostility of the Buddhist clergy towards him. During his stay, he heard tell of another region called Greater Tibet, or the 'Kingdom of Utsang', situated a month and a half's walk away to the east. His advice was to try and approach it from the southern side of the Himalayas, from the direction of Bengal.

The country had become a theocracy in 1642, with the 5th Dalai Lama at its head, and in 1661 the first two Europeans to officially enter Lhasa were Father Johann

Grueber and Father Albert d'Orville. The former was Austrian, the latter Belgian, and they were based in

Missionaries such as Grueber, Desideri and Andrade (above, aged 54, portrait painted in India, 1634) provided the first accounts of the country and also of its 'king', in fact the 5th Dalai Lama, who had built the Potala. Grueber took back a sketch of it (below left). His descriptions of Lhasa, which had recently become the capital of Tibet, were the first eyewitness account, and their publication by Kirchner in 1677 created a great deal of interest in this strange country. Among the illustrations is that of 'Two idols in the town of Barantola' (opposite), representing the historical Buddha and the eleven-headed Avalokiteshvara, before whom two Tibetans are bowing in reverence.

THE QUEST OF THE WEST 83

China but had found it impossible to get back to Europe by ship. They therefore decided to go to India by crossing China. They reached Lhasa on 8 October 1661, and stayed there for over two months. Their notes and sketches were published in Latin in 1677 by Athanasius Kircher, and are especially notable for including the earliest references to the Dalai Lama and the Potala.

At the beginning of the 18th century both Jesuits and Capuchins, simultaneously and without prior knowledge of each other's intentions, set out to establish missions in Tibet: this subsequently led to a dispute over rights of anteriority. The Capuchins chose the more accessible and in fact the shorter route from the south of the Himalayas, whereas the Jesuits followed Antonio de Andrade's arduous route from the west, across the high Tibetan plateaux of Ladakh. Their journey to the 'third and great

Despite the efforts of these pioneering missionaries, the West still knew little about Tibet. In effect, the Christian church proved incapable of imposing itself on this part of the world, and so tried not to lose face: firstly, it sought to discredit Buddhist beliefs and practices, which it suddenly condemned as barbarous and primitive, although previously it had presented them as being similar to Christianity; secondly, it divulged only a tiny part of the accounts written by its missionaries. It must be said that the reports of these audacious travellers

Tibet' was gruelling and took them more than seven months. In 1716 the Capuchin father Orazio Della Penna and the Jesuit fathers Emmanuel Freyre and Ippolito Desideri all found themselves together in Lhasa. Even if they were not exactly enthusiastic over this forced cohabitation in the same city, Desideri and Della Penna soon came to have a great deal of respect for each other, and set about studying Tibetan together. Their aim was

were unanimous in their praise of the spirit of tolerance mixed with curiosity shown by the Tibetan clergy, who allowed them to live in their country and even establish missions there.

to convert people, not by ridiculing the Buddhist theories of the great lamas, but by refuting them. They were both admitted to Sera Monastery, near Lhasa.

Desideri left Tibet in 1721, and on his return to Rome he wrote an account of his travels which was not published until 1904, perhaps because the Church did not want to reveal too openly the tensions that existed between the Capuchins and the Jesuits. His book was ultimately to gain wide – though long delayed – recognition as a remarkable work by a scholar, geographer and explorer, and it made a major contribution to a better understanding of Tibet and of Lhasa. He described the workings of the government, and also the intense trading activity in Lhasa – a crossroads where all the arts and cultures of Asia came together. He was present during the Dzungar Mongol invasion of 1720, and witnessed the political changes that took place before and after the death of the 6th Dalai Lama. As for Della Penna, he spent sixteen years in Tibet. During this time the Manchus undermined the

Exaggerated images became popular in the West ('Burning of a lama's body', above, late 18th century), but some drawings were of genuine ethnographic interest (below, left and opposite).

monks' trust in all things Western, and the last missions soon closed.

Emissaries and adventurers

During the second half of the 18th century, missionaries were replaced by travellers whose main aim was to find new avenues for trade. The East India Company, particularly well situated in Bengal, was keen to open up new markets, but in order to do this, political intervention was sometimes necessary. In 1774 the Governor-General of India, Warren Hastings, decided to send a mission to Tibet in order to negotiate future Anglo-Tibetan relations. George Bogle, a young Scotsman, was ordered to go to Shigatse, rather than to Lhasa, because the young Dalai Lama was only fifteen, and so the real spiritual and political

In 1759, the *Alphabetum Tibetanum* was published in Rome by the Congregation of the Propagation of the Faith, which in 1703 had sent the Capuchins to evangelize Tibet. Largely based on letters written by the Capuchin Della Penna, this book contained remarkably accurate illustrations. The Tibetan liturgical objects were well reproduced, in particular the prayer wheels and flags that so intrigued the missionaries. In 1740

power lay with the 6th Panchen Lama – one of the most important in the lineage, who lived in Tashilunpo Monastery near Shigatse. At first Bogle was disappointed by the monotony of the landscape, but he gradually grew interested in the people. He became a personal friend of the Panchen Lama, studied the language and customs of the country, and married a Tibetan woman, but he was to die prematurely in 1781. Although his mission was not a commercial success, his own account of it– which was not published until a century later, in 1876 – contains valuable information about this period of Tibetan history.

In 1783, in recognition of the 4th Panchen Lama, Hastings sent a second mission led by Captain Samuel Turner. His account, published in 1800, was used as a reference work for more than a century, since it provided

Della Penna returned to Tibet, accompanied by Fra Cassiano da Macerata, who produced a journal with sketches of great historical and ethnographical interest (above, a procession of monks, Gyantse). The Capuchin mission to Tibet ended in 1741 through lack of financial support and because of the hostility of the Buddhist clergy towards the missionaries – in marked contrast to their attitudes of the previous century.

clear explanations of relations between Tashilunpo, Lhasa and the Manchu dynasty of the Qing.

A forbidden land

It was just as the colonial powers were building their empires that the Tibetan government decided in 1810 to close Tibet and Lhasa to all foreigners. The Tibetans were encouraged in this policy by the Manchus, who ruled China and who saw this as a means of protecting their own relations with Tibet against all foreign influence. Later the British took the same line, because among other things they wanted to establish trade relations with Tibet while also warding off any Russian interference. Thus it was that at the beginning of the 19th century Tibet became a forbidden land or, in the imagination of the West, a forbidden fruit that became more and more of a temptation.

In the course of this century, however, three travellers succeeded without too much difficulty in crossing Tibet and staying in the 'Forbidden City'. It may have been because he was a doctor that Thomas Manning was allowed to accompany a Chinese general whom he met in 1811 at the frontier. His true destination seems to have been China itself, for which he had a true passion, and his descriptions of Tibet and of Lhasa are rather negative: the climate was harsh, the country very dirty and completely under the control of the Chinese, who were extremely civilized compared to the Tibetans. Apart from the Potala palace, which was more impressive than he

Although eastern Tibet (Kham and Amdo) were relatively accessible – a lot of Westerners explored and stayed in the region during the 19th and early 20th centuries – Central Tibet became out of bounds. Nevertheless Fathers Huc and Gabet (opposite below, in Chinese dress, 1852) reached Lhasa in 1846. Huc wrote of Lhasa, its monks and its mendicant pilgrims (above, painting by H. A. Oldfield, 1852).

had imagined, he was disappointed by the city itself: 'There is nothing striking, nothing pleasing in its appearance. The habitations are begrimed with smut and dirt. The avenues are full of dogs....' The journal of Manning, the first Englishman to reach Lhasa, was published in 1876.

In 1846, two French Lazarists, Father Evariste Huc and Father Joseph Gabet, reached Lhasa after a gruelling journey of nearly two years across China, the Gobi Desert, Mongolia and north-eastern Tibet. Their primary purpose was to convert the Mongols, but in the course of their work and through various chance meetings they began to grow attracted to the holy city. They took advantage of an unexpected meeting with the caravan of some emissaries from the Dalai Lama who were returning from the court at Beijing, and joined up with them. On 29 January 1846 they entered Lhasa. Although Huc and Gabet were both missionaries, they were also good observers. Their account of Tibetan culture is precise and invaluable. In particular, they lay emphasis on the bustle in the centre of Lhasa, and on the ethnic diversity to be found there. As the report continues, the two priests

In 1791 the Nepalese Gurkhas once more invaded Tibet and ransacked Tashilunpo Monastery in Shigatse (above, mausoleum at Tashilunpo, Samuel Davis, 1783). The Qing dynasty reacted sharply, and on the pretext of protecting Lhasa against the 'English expansionists' – whom they accused of being behind the invasion – they pushed for a total ban on Westerners in eastern Tibet.

Westerners found many different reasons for crossing the Tibetan borders. At the beginning of the 19th century, a Hungarian, Csoma de Körös, the first Tibetologist, spent some years studying Tibetan at Zanskar and Kinnaur in the Himalayas. In 1890 Henri d'Orléans and his companion Gabriel Bonvalot set out to contradict the rumours and prove that Huc and Gabet had truly reached Tibet; the two explorers ended their journey not far from Lhasa. Henri d'Orléans took back an extensive photographic record of Tibet. (Above, women with braided hair, Amdo, 1890).

make less and less effort to hide their aversion to the Chinese and their liking for the Mongols and the Tibetans who had made them very welcome. They never tried to conceal their own foreignness, and were finally expelled from Lhasa, taking more than three months to go back across eastern Tibet. As soon as it was published, their report was an outstanding success, and when, in 1890, French duke Henri d'Orléans set out for Asia, having decided to go to Tibet, he paid tribute to Father Huc: 'Always and everywhere we have been surprised by the accuracy of the French missionary's descriptions…'. It was, however, after these unwanted visits that the Manchus and Tibetans decided to completely exclude all foreigners.

'The Great Game'

The second half of the 19th century was an era of intense rivalry between Britain and Russia for control of Central Asia and Tibet. Of the Russians, the most resolute was Colonel Nikolai Prejevalsky of the Imperial Army, who led an expedition to northern Tibet in 1872. In 1879 he organized another expedition across Mongolia and northern Tibet in order to enter Lhasa, but he was stopped 250 km north of the capital. He died in 1883 on the shore of Lake Issyk Kul in the Tien Shan Mountains, once more on his way to Lhasa.

The British for their part mounted a campaign of 'clandestine cartography'. They employed some Indian agents, who set off for Tibet disguised as pilgrims, having first been taught to note down the topography. From 1865 to the end of the 1880s, these pandits – the most famous of whom were Nain Singh, Kishen Singh and the heroic Kintup – risked their lives to provide the British with a vast quantity of scientific information. The pandit Sarat Chandra Das, immortalized in Rudyard Kipling's *Kim* under the name of Mookerjee, was in Central Tibet from 1879 to 1881 and wrote a Tibetan-English dictionary which is still used as a reference book today.

Everyone with a spirit of adventure began to launch the craziest schemes in order to get themselves to Central Tibet and the Forbidden City. Most of them never got anywhere near, often being stopped at Nagchu, the gateway to Central Tibet 300 km north of Lhasa, either at the guard posts in eastern Tibet or by the British guards on the foothills of the Himalayas. Virtually all these expeditions ended in failure. This was certainly the case for the English missionary Annie Taylor, and for the Englishman Henry Savage

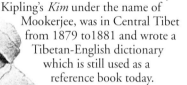

Born in Chittagong, India, Sarat Chandra Das (left, mounted on a yak, 1881) was both a scholar and a British spy in Tibet. The British were increasingly concerned about the supposed influence of the Russian empire on Tibet, especially when they heard in 1901 about the mission of Dordjieff (above), a Buddhist monk of Buryat origin, who acted as a go-between for Tsar Nicholas II and Lhasa, where he had been studying since 1880. Accused of being an *éminence grise* paid by the Russians to influence the 13th Dalai Lama, he was one of the reasons for the British expedition of 1904.

Landor, who was imprisoned in 1897 in southern Tibet. Two expeditions came to a tragic end in eastern Tibet: that of French explorer Dutreuil de Rhins in 1893, and that of the Dutch missionary Petrus Rijnhart, who was accompanied by his Canadian wife Susie and their baby son Charlie in 1898. Only his wife survived the adventure.

Worried by what they considered to be the empire-building ambitions of the Russians, the British launched an expedition to Tibet in 1904 under the leadership of Colonel Francis Younghusband. This led to the death of

An official from Lhasa (on the left) accompanied the Abbot of Tashilunpo to southern Tibet in order to negotiate with the Younghusband expedition, which was threatening Shigatse and Lhasa. A servant is standing behind the lama, next to a little altar on which there are ewers and sacrificial

a thousand Tibetans, and by the time the British army reached Lhasa, the 13th Dalai Lama had fled to Mongolia. Perceval Landon, the *Times* correspondent who accompanied the mission, observed Tibetan society and took home sketches and photographs. He wrote: 'I have said much in these volumes to the discredit of Lamaism, and I have said it with deliberation and conviction; but this panorama of Lhasa batters down

cakes. There are cups of tea on the low tables. Salted butter tea is a staple drink, and is ritually served and drunk; it is even given to enemies (photo Jean-Claude White, 1903).

helplessly the prejudices of a quieter hour. Lamaism may be an engine of oppression, but its victims do not protest.... To Lamaism alone we owe it that when at last the sight of the farthest goal of all travel burst upon our eyes, it was worthy, full worthy, of all the rumour and glamour and romance with which in the imaginings of man it has been invested for so many years.'

All these men who set out to conquer Tibet gradually found themselves being conquered by it, starting with Colonels Waddell and Younghusband, whose initial scepticism gave way to the same lyrical enthusiasm. L.A.Waddell, the expedition's head doctor and a devout Scottish Presbyterian, wrote; 'Wreathed in the romance of centuries, Lhasa, the secret citadel of the "undying" Grand Lama, has stood shrouded in impenetrable mystery on the Roof-of-the-World, alluring yet defying our most adventurous travellers to enter her closed gates.'

Younghusband left Lhasa with thoughts that were to change his whole way of life: 'I was insensibly suffused with an almost intoxicating sense of elation and good-will.... Never again could I think evil, or ever again be at enmity with any man.'

In 1907, and then again in 1909–10, the French explorer Jacques Bacot crossed eastern Tibet, which at the time was ruled by the Manchus. He took an ethnological viewpoint, and his account bears witness to the disasters caused by the war between the Chinese and the Tibetans. The poet Victor Segalen, who was in China at the same time as his friend Bacot, experienced the fascination of Tibet in a mystical manner. He never succeeded in reaching Tibet itself, but wrote a whole collection of poems in its praise: 'Lha-sa, your roofs of

Camps punctuated the life of travellers in Tibet. Settlements were rare, and pack animals had to be fed. Water and, if possible, wood were necessities, as seen here in Kham (photo Jacques Bacot, Yarlung valley, 1909). On arrival at the camp, the mules and yaks were unsaddled, and a fire lit in order to prepare tea and food, provide warmth, and frighten away wild animals. All Westerners took their own food and personal effects with them. Some of them even travelled in style. At Christmas 1903 the members of the Younghusband expedition complained that their champagne was undrinkable at -40 degrees C.

'I rejoiced at the thought that I was the first European to wander in the solitude of those mountains, where the only tracks were those trodden by yaks, wild donkeys and antelopes....'
Those were the words of Sven Hedin (1865–1952), the famous Swedish explorer who crossed the whole of western Tibet between 1906 and 1909, and accomplished extraordinary feats of cartography and orography: he discovered and named the Transhimalayan range, the sources of the Indus, the Brahmaputra and the Sutlej, not far from the sacred Mount Kailash. An artist and a painter, he depicted in the brightest of colours the landscapes, villages, temples and people – such as the women from western Tibet with their festive headdresses (left), a monk pushing the door of a mausoleum in Tashilunpo (opposite, below), and the little monasteries near the Tsangpo river (opposite, above). Towards the end of his life, Hedin shocked his colleagues and compatriots with his Nazi sympathies, but nevertheless left behind some remarkable maps and books.

gold, o Lha-sa, and yet it is over, finished, it is ended, sung and played, too distant...too late, Lha-sa, I shall not go to Lha-sa!'

First White Woman to Enter Fork

Rare visits by Westerners

After the fall of the Manchu empire in 1911, the 13th Dalai Lama proclaimed the independence of Tibet in 1912 – a declaration that was not recognized by the government of republican China. The only Westerners who were legally allowed to travel to Central Tibet at the beginning of the century were British representatives posted at Sikkim. Of these, David MacDonald and Sir Charles Bell – the only foreigners allowed into Lhasa in 1921 – became acute observers of Tibetan culture, and it was their writings that at last rendered this culture

In 1924, at the age of 56, Alexandra David-Néel (opposite) reached Lhasa after an exhausting journey over thousands of miles. Disguised as a beggar, she was the first European woman to enter Lhasa. She too succumbed to the charms of Tibet: 'I remain enchanted… I was on the edge of a mystery…Yes, I shall dream about it for a long time, all my life, and a bond will remain between me and this land of clouds and snows.'

accessible to Europeans. In 1927 it was a Frenchwoman, Alexandra David-Néel, who achieved a resounding success in Europe and the US with the publication of her book *My Journey to Lhasa*. She helped greatly to popularize an image of Tibet in the West that reached beyond the rather restricted circle of Orientalists and diplomats.

Other British representatives made brief visits to Tibet, but one of them, Hugh Richardson, stayed in Lhasa for eight years, from 1936 to 1940, and from 1946 to 1950. He was a fine photographer and an expert on Tibetan society and history, and on his retirement from diplomatic service he became an eminent Tibetologist and a fervent supporter of Tibetan independence. There were two other Britons who were employed as radio operators: Reg Fox, who arrived in Lhasa in 1937 and married a Tibetan girl, and Robert Ford. In 1950 the latter watched in despair as the Chinese army took Chamdo, a town in eastern Tibet that commands the route from eastern Tibet to Lhasa. He was taken prisoner and spent five years in Chinese gaols for espionage.

dden City of Tibet

There were also some non-British Westerners who succeeded in climbing the bureaucratic fence and spent weeks or even months in Tibet. At the beginning of the 1930s the American naturalist Brooke Dolan went twice to eastern Tibet, accompanied by a young German zoologist, Ernst Schäffer. In 1938–39, Schäffer went to Central Tibet, this time with a team of scientists who were all members of the SS and were financed by Himmler. The latter was fascinated by Tibet, and wanted to prove that the land of Shambhala truly existed, and that Tibet was one of the cradles of mankind. The expedition returned with a film, photographs of 2,000

•The town is not very interesting. I've had my fill of visits to monasteries; I've seen so many! …The palace of the Dalai Lama… has nothing very special about it [opposite, photo by Hugh Richardson]. In town, instead of exotic objects, the shopkeepers lay out piles of aluminium saucepans.•

Alexandra David-Néel, letter to her husband.

The Second World War brought the first official American mission to Tibet (left, the Tolstoy mission between the Upper Yangtse and the Upper Mekong, 1942). The Cuttings, rich financiers from New York, had links with the 13th and 14th Dalai Lamas, and had already visited Lhasa in 1935 and 1937. Since the beginning of the century, a handful of American missionaries had also been living in Amdo and Kham, in eastern Tibet, and had set up small schools and health centres.

Tibetans, the anthropometric measurements of 376 people, and some casts of Tibetan heads.

Brooke Dolan himself returned to Central Tibet from Sikkim in 1942, during the war. He was then a lieutenant in the OSS (precursor of the CIA), and was accompanied by a young OSS captain, Ilya Tolstoy, grandson of the great Russian novelist. This was the first American mission to Tibet. Their official task was to negotiate with the Tibetan government for permission to fly planes carrying war equipment through Tibetan airspace. In fact, however, they really wanted to know if they could construct a road across Tibet. The two officers spent several months in Lhasa, and finally left for China at the end of the winter of 1942–43, travelling via north-eastern Tibet.

The great Italian Tibetologist Giuseppe Tucci, accompanied by the photographer Petro Mele and the young Fosco Maraini, managed to make eight scientific expeditions to Tibet between 1933 and 1948, the year when he finally got to Lhasa with authorization from the Tibetan government. The Italians moved on to Tsaparang and Tholing in western Tibet, where they met the lama Anagarika Govinda – a Buddhist originally from Germany – and his wife Li Gotami, who had gone there in 1947–48. They all returned with invaluable photographic records of temples, paintings and statues that have since been destroyed.

The general public got a taste of everyday life in Lhasa in the middle of the 20th century through the adventures of two Austrian mountaineers, Heinrich Harrer and Peter Aufschnaiter. Having escaped from

a prison camp in India, they crossed the Himalayan barrier, and after wandering for months across the high plateaux, they reached Lhasa in 1946. The 14th and present Dalai Lama was then an adolescent who was extremely curious to know about the outside world, and the two men won his confidence. Harrer's book *Seven Years in Tibet* became an international bestseller during the 1950s, and was made into a successful film in 1994.

Tourists, students, the 'tolerant years'

After 1951 and the Chinese invasion, or 'peaceful liberation', the bamboo curtain fell over Tibet, which became more inaccessible than ever except for a few envoys from 'brother countries' whose tenets followed the Communist Party line. The Cultural Revolution increased this isolation, and the Red Guards caused destruction with impunity.

In 1981 the Tibet Autonomous Region (*Xizang* in Chinese) – founded in 1965 and incorporating

In summer 1939, at Kumbum Monastery in Amdo, a caravan (below) prepares to accompany the young 14th Dalai Lama to Lhasa. He recalls in his memoirs: 'The party was large. Not only did it consist of my parents and my brother...[but] a number of pilgrims came too. There were also several government officials in attendance, together with a great number of muleteers and scouts.... The journey to Lhasa took three months. I remember very little detail apart from a great sense of wonder at everything I saw.'

central and western Tibet – was opened up again under the iron rule of the Chinese, who realized that Tibet was a potential tourist attraction and as such, a potentially considerable source of income. Groups of tourists were encouraged to come, and countless individuals undertook the extremely arduous journey. A cautious form of liberalism began to emerge, through the efforts of Hu Yaobang (who was swiftly deposed by the Party) and the 10th Panchen Lama, who died in 1989. These were the so-called 'tolerant years'.

In the second half of the 19th century, Europe developed a passion for mysticism which crystallized around the name 'Tibet'. Theosophists, inspired by Helena Blavatsky and Georgei Gurdjieff, were convinced that the land was a source of mystical

Demonstrations for Tibetan independence took place in Lhasa in 1987, 1988, and 1989, and led to riots that were bloodily suppressed. Hu Jintao, then head of the Communist Party in Tibet, brought in martial law in 1989. Once again it became increasingly difficult to travel to Tibet except in supervised groups and at an exorbitant cost. Nevertheless, despite these hostile political conditions, Western tourists still flocked to Tibet, which then swiftly set up the infrastructures to accommodate them – including air links. In 2000, there were 132,000 foreign visitors to the country.

In the name of evangelism

Among these crowds of foreigners were new waves of missionaries, mainly evangelical. These groups, based in USA or Hong Kong, saw Tibet and Bhutan as the 'last

knowledge, and Walter Evans-Wentz, the first translator of the *Tibetan Book of the Dead* (1925), was a theosophist. James Hilton's novel *Lost Horizon* (1933), which Frank Capra filmed in 1937 (film poster above), was influenced by these ideas, and describes a paradisal land called Shangri-La, hidden in the heart of the Himalayas. In modern times, the Chinese have given the name Shangri-La to a valley in eastern Tibet.

frontier', the last bastion against Christianity. Even though at the end of the 19th and beginning of the 20th centuries there had been Catholic and Protestant missionaries in eastern Tibet, as well as priests from foreign missions on the borders of Tibet and Yunnan, the number of Tibetan converts was negligible. In 1986 the Chinese government began to recruit English teachers, which presented the missionaries with a golden opportunity, and a large number of so-called 'teachers' duly arrived with Bibles in their bags. Similarly, during the mid-1990s the University of Tibet offered courses in Tibetan to foreigners, and some of the American and Korean students were also missionaries. China turned a blind eye to their activities, because the government tended to take a positive view of anything that might remove the Tibetans from Buddhist influence, but the Tibetan people themselves seemed to have little desire to be converted.

Conversely, the West developed a passion for Tibetan Buddhism – as propagated by the spiritual teachers who went into exile during the 1950s – and interest in Tibetan culture increased, especially through the charismatic figure of the 14th Dalai Lama, who won the Nobel Peace Prize in 1989. The 'fashion' for Tibet was spread by the media, film stars and publicity, and the New Age movement adopted some of the values of Tibetan Buddhism. But historical and political realities were eclipsed by these religious trends and by international commerce. Once more, as at the time of Herodotus, the West only saw that part of Tibet which nourished its fantasies of the moment; Tibet remained a prisoner of the image of Shangri-La, the paradisal valley invented in 1933 by James Hilton in his novel *Lost Horizon*.

Countless artists have been fascinated by Tibet and its myths. The films *Seven Years in Tibet* (1994) and *Kundun* (1997) were seen by huge audiences. The comic book *Tintin in Tibet* (1960) is one of the most popular in the Tintin series, and is fairly well researched, although it does reuse some of the old clichés like the levitating monk shown here. Its Chinese edition, under the title *Tintin in Chinese Tibet* (2001), was at first withdrawn from sale, but has recently been

reissued under its original title.

'We must be ready to defend ourselves. Otherwise our spiritual and cultural traditions will be completely eradicated. Even the names of the Dalai and Panchen Lamas will be erased.... The monasteries will be looted and destroyed, and the monks and nuns killed or chased away.... The birthrights and property of the people will be stolen. We will become like slaves to our conquerors, and will be made to wander helplessly like beggars. Everyone will be forced to live in misery, and the days and nights will pass slowly, and with great suffering and terror.'

Testament of the 13th Dalai Lama, 1931

CHAPTER 5

INVASION AND COLONIZATION: TIBET TODAY

Soldiers and the Chinese flag in front of the Potala Palace (opposite); statues destroyed by the Chinese (right): the words of the 13th Dalai Lama ring out like a prophecy.

In 1947 the Tibetan government sent a trade mission to the West. The Americans and the British stamped the Tibetan passports with visas, and thereby recognized the independence of Tibet. In July 1949, with a Communist seizure of power imminent in China, the Tibetan government expelled all Chinese, including traders. But the new Chinese government saw Tibet as an integral part of their country, and Chinese radio announced that Tibet must be 'liberated from the British imperialist yoke'. Isolated by its own foreign policy during the last two hundred years, Tibet received no support from the West – not even from Great Britain. Furthermore, the USSR took China's side, and India recognized China's suzerainty over Tibet.

The 'liberation' of Tibet

This sad period forces us to believe that the Dalai Lama and the Panchen Lama – two adolescents who knew nothing of the modern world and its politics – were manipulated by their respective entourages, whose primary concerns were to protect their own status. Indeed, the very young Panchen Lama (born in Qinghai

In October 1951, thousands of soldiers of the People's Liberation Army marched into Lhasa from Sichuan and Qinghai. They had come 3000 km through this inhospitable land, galvanized by Mao, with orders to 'peacefully' liberate the country from the 'imperialist yoke' and its people from slavery, so that they could be reunited with the 'mother country'. The problem of the Chinese in Lhasa was not the resistance of the Tibetans, but logistics: how were thousands of soldiers to be fed and housed? But the soldiers themselves were disciplined and earned the admiration of the local people.

in 1938), or rather his advisers, did believe at the time that the Dalai Lama and his court at Lhasa could benefit from the situation, and it was they who sent a message to China asking them to send in the People's Liberation Army (PLA).

On 1 January 1950, Radio Beijing announced that Tibet was about to be liberated. Finally in Lhasa fear began to mount, but even then the danger had been underestimated. The troops were reinforced on the eastern frontiers of Tibet, and the Chinese invaded the whole of Kham, reaching the Yangtse river. The Tibetan government was incapable of responding, due to a lack of trained soldiers and a pro- and anti-Chinese split within the monastic and aristocratic hierarchy. On 7 October 1950, 40,000 Chinese soldiers, on orders from Deng Xiaoping, political commissioner for the army at Sichuan, crossed the river. Under the command of Ngapo Ngawang Jigme they took Chamdo, the great city of the east, on 17 October after three weeks of fighting. Eight thousand Tibetan soldiers were killed. The route to Central Tibet was now open. Of course India protested, but the West abandoned Tibet to its fate, being more concerned about the situation in Korea. El Salvador took Tibet's case to the UN in November 1950, but without success. Tibet was regarded as an internal affair of China – a refrain that has been repeated many times over the last fifty years.

Propaganda photos from 1950–51 show Tibetans giving an enthusiastic welcome to the Chinese army. Here in Kangting (Dartsendo/Tachienlu) in Kham, a delegation of women carrying flowers and banners greet the Liberation Army. In order to win the people over, the soldiers were given strict orders: not to occupy houses without permission from the inhabitants; not to kill birds or fish; to respect customs and all sacred objects; not to allow any female staff to enter the monasteries. This public relations exercise also extended to the nobles and the clergy. Mao's orders were to 'make every possible effort by all appropriate means to win over the Dalai Lama and the majority of the upper classes, and to isolate the minority of bad elements in order to achieve the long-term objective of transforming the economy and politics of Tibet gradually and without bloodshed.'

During this time the Dalai Lama, at the age of fifteen, was enthroned in Lhasa as head of state. Ngapo, now vice-President of the Committee of Liberation, called on the Tibetan government to negotiate with China. This was a parody of compromise. It was impossible for the Tibetans to oppose the Liberation Army, and the Chinese only wanted to negotiate in order to justify themselves to the Tibetans and to the international community. A high-level Tibetan delegation, led by Ngapo, was sent to Beijing in April 1951. The text of the agreement was already fixed; no negotiation was possible. After some equivocation, the Tibetan delegation unwillingly signed the '17-Point Agreement' on 23 May 1951, handing Tibet over to the Chinese. The 1st article stated that the Tibetan people would return to the family of the mother country, the People's Republic of China. It was a clear but contradictory statement: clear because it announced that Tibet was now a province of China; contradictory because it implied that Tibet was not in fact part of China.

Chinese policy in action

In autumn 1951 the Liberation Army reached Central Tibet, approaching simultaneously from the east and the

Mao invited the 10th Panchen Lama (on his right) and the 14th Dalai Lama (on his left) to make an official visit to China, and he received them in Beijing in 1954 (above). The young Dalai Lama was at first charmed by Mao's conciliatory words and apparent interest in Tibet. He remarked how kind Mao had been, and formed a genuine respect for him. On the occasion of their final meeting, however, Mao dropped his mask and said that although he understood the Dalai Lama's point of view, he regarded religion as a poison. It has, he said, two faults: it destroys a race, and it slows down a country's progress.

north-west: 'On 26 October the People's Army of Liberation marched into the interior of Tibet, and the Tibetan people were liberated from imperialist aggression and returned to the great family of the People's Republic of China' (Xinhua, the Chinese news agency). When the Liberation Army reached Lhasa, it marched in orderly fashion, with red flags and portraits of Mao, parading before an anxious and bewildered people that had little knowledge of what was going on. Within a few months, 20,000 Chinese soldiers were stationed in Lhasa – half the city's population at the time.

For some years the Chinese behaved themselves, and gave gifts to the nobles, many of whom came over onto their side. Schools and hospitals were provided. At the same time army garrisons were set up all over Tibet, virtually locking it in. Roads linking Tibet to China, finished in 1954, facilitated the transport of troops.

Also in 1954, the Dalai Lama and Panchen Lama were invited to Beijing, where they were received with great ceremony by Zhou Enlai and Mao Zedong. The teenage Dalai Lama was quite charmed by Mao, who made soothing comments about religion, right up until their last meeting, when Mao told him that in fact religion was a poison. On his return journey in 1955, the Dalai Lama could see only too well the hold that the Chinese had on his native province, Amdo. Away from Lhasa, the Communist reforms were well and truly underway. The monasteries had gradually been stripped, and the Tibetans slowly realized that they had no say in their own affairs.

In 1956 the 'Preparatory Commission for the Autonomous Region of Tibet' was created, with General Ngapo as its

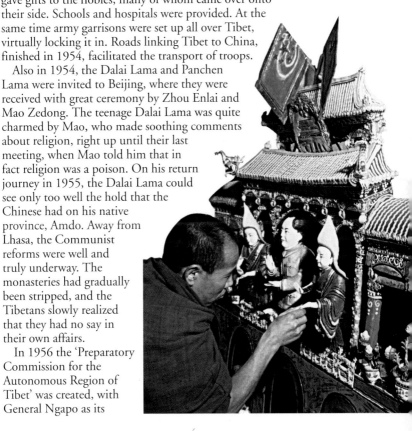

Mao's cult of personality reached Tibet and was adapted to local customs. Below, an East Tibetan monk places Mao between two great lamas of the Gelugpa school in a model of the Forbidden City's temple, with Chinese flags flying from the top.

secretary, and this culminated in the creation of the Tibet Autonomous Region in September 1965. The Dalai Lama was its president, but he was only a puppet. Power now lay exclusively with the Committee of the Communist Party.

Rebellion and the flight of the Dalai Lama

Infuriated by the Chinese reforms, attacks on their religion, and the fact that they were even forced to feed the occupying armies, the Tibetans of Amdo and Kham rebelled in 1955. These people, often divided in the past, now united against the invader. Even monks took up arms. There was now a bloody guerrilla war with the Chinese. At

this point the US, furious with the Chinese for their role in Korea, began to take a new interest in Tibet. The CIA ran secret training courses in the US and delivered arms and radio equipment to the guerrillas in the east. This operation did not officially end until 1971, when Henry Kissinger went to Beijing to try and normalize relations between China and the US.

In 1956 Beijing sent 150,000 men to Kham, supported by air raids. Tibetan resistance was shattered by these 'balls of fire' falling from the sky, and the

The Tibetan flag became a symbol of resistance and of a free Tibet (top). The monks were also involved in resistance. They were forced to surrender their weapons after the 1959 rebellion in Lhasa. (The photo above is probably a reconstruction.)

Chinese army regained control of Kham in a bloodbath. Reprisals, particularly against the clergy, were horrific, and whole villages were razed.

No Tibetan in Lhasa would or could grasp the situation. Neither did news travel abroad. Chinese propaganda claimed that the Dalai Lama had been authorized to go to India to celebrate the 2,500th anniversary of the birth of the Buddha. Nehru met him but could give him no hope or support other than to advise him to cooperate with the Chinese. The Dalai Lama returned to Lhasa when rumours of a general uprising in Central Tibet began to grow. In 1958 tensions became even greater when thousands of East Tibetans arrived in Lhasa with news of more disasters.

No photos of the Lhasa rebellion are available. For one thing, no foreign journalists were present; the Chinese did not want to show the Tibetan people in revolt at a time when they were supposed to be grateful for their 'liberation'. However, there are some rare photos of the surrender, for these prove that the 'dangerous element of the feudal society' were defeated. Against the

On 10 March 1959 the crisis was heightened when the Chinese authorities issued an unusual invitation to the Dalai Lama: he was to come alone to the Chinese camp to attend a theatrical performance. When he refused to accept the invitation, the Chinese decided to 'liberate' him from reactionary forces. Having got wind of this, the Dalai Lama fled with his entourage and an escort of Khampa guerrillas during the night of 16–17 March 1959. On 30 March 1959 he arrived in India, where Nehru gave him political asylum. The Chinese did not

background of the Potala, a line of men walk single file, their hands in the air. Their clothes suggest that they are nobles, but ordinary people – including women – also took part in the fighting. This photo may be a reconstruction for propaganda purposes.

learn of his escape straight away, and were taken aback by the scale of the insurrection.

From 20 to 22 March 1959, Lhasa was ablaze, and the fighting became all the more bloody and all the more one-sided as the Chinese brought their tanks into action. Estimates of the Tibetan death toll varied from 2,000 to 10,000, while some 4,000 were taken prisoner. Between 1959 and 1960, faced with such violent repression, at least 80,000 Tibetans fled either to India, following the Dalai Lama, or to Nepal. Poverty-stricken, weak, and unused to the Indian climate, many died of tuberculosis or diarrhoea in the camps that were set up by the High Commission for Refugees (HCR) and the Indian government.

In lay clothing (below) the Dalai Lama escaped from Lhasa on horseback with a hundred friends and relatives and four hundred resistance fighters. The Chinese did not learn of his escape until 48 hours later, and attacked Norbulingka, where they thought he would still be. The fugitives took fifteen days to cross the mountains and reach Tawang in India.

A nation in exile

Tibet suddenly hit the headlines in the West. The Dalai Lama immediately gave a press conference denouncing the 17-Point Agreement, and the UN passed a resolution condemning Chinese policy in Tibet. The Indian government gave assistance to the Tibetans, and put the ancient colonial town of McLeod Ganj, above Dharamsala, at the disposal of the Dalai Lama. In 1960 a

'There was nothing dramatic about the crossing of the frontier. The country was equally wild on the other side and uninhabited. I saw it in a daze of sickness and weariness and unhappiness deeper than I can express.'

14th Dalai Lama

government-in-exile was established, and the Tibetans began to get organized, with Indian and international aid. In the course of the years and with a good deal of financial support, there gradually came into being a Tibet in exile, with administrative centres, children's villages, monasteries, libraries and records offices. But after 45 years of iron rule by China, Tibetans must still risk their lives to cross the Himalayas.

Democratic reforms and the working classes

Since 1959 Tibetan culture has suffered numerous attempts to destroy it. The years that followed the flight of the Dalai Lama were appalling. There were bloody reprisals against the people, compulsory Communist

Nehru, the Indian Prime Minister (below, with the Dalai Lama), granted asylum to the Dalai Lama and the Tibetan refugees, but this gesture put him in a difficult position with China, who accused him of 'imperialism and expansionism'. Nehru could not defend Tibet against China, and so the Dalai Lama placed his hopes in the UN, which in October 1959 passed a resolution upholding the rights of the Tibetans, but this had no effect.

OVER 65,000 TIBETANS EXTERMINATED
Dalai Lama appeals to civilised world

indoctrination, redistribution of land to the 'working classes', public sessions of 'criticism' which often degenerated into torture, annihilation of monastic life, and the removal of works of art to China. The aim was to 'exterminate the reactionary forces of Tibet', to 'emancipate the slaves'. 'Democratic reform', with the aid of these Tibetan slaves, was completed in 1961. Famine was everywhere, as in China itself. Family and religious structures collapsed, and 'counter-revolutionaries' and 'reactionaries' were systematically rounded up and sent for re-education at labour camps – the *laogai* – where many of them died. The exact number of these prisoners is not known, but some estimates put it at 70,000.

The Panchen Lama, who had remained in Tibet, appeared to sanction this situation, and

The first refugees reached the Indian plains after travelling across the Himalayas in appalling conditions. They were placed in camps, and had to endure the humid heat of India, in stark contrast to the dry cold that they were used to. Still dressed in their heavy Tibetan garments, here they seem bewildered by the climate, fatigue, grief, fear of the future – their faces locked in an expression of uncertainty as they wait. All they know is that the Dalai Lama is also in this country, which for them is the land of the Buddha. Many died of dysentery or tuberculosis. Once in India, the Tibetans fashioned a way of life which they thought would only be temporary. Other Tibetans dispersed to Nepal, Australia, Europe, Canada and the United States. The nation set up a government-in-exile, and since 2001 has had a Prime Minister elected by universal suffrage, Samdhong Rinpoche. Tibetan Buddhism is enjoying great popularity today, not only in the West. The Chinese in Taiwan and the diaspora all flock to the lamas. But refugees continue to arrive from Tibet, and the 'temporary' way of life has now gone on for fifty years.

held the post of Vice-President of the People's Consultative Assembly. In fact, however, in 1962 at the age of 24 he sent a petition to Mao, vehemently denouncing Chinese policy in Tibet. Early in 1964, having made a public speech in Lhasa calling for the Dalai Lama to return to the throne, he was submitted to a terrible session of 'criticism', sent to prison in China, and not released until 1978.

Tibetans indoctrinated by the Chinese duly took up executive positions in the Party and became cogs in the new administrative machinery. In 1965 the Tibet Autonomous Region became a reality, but it represented no more than a third of cultural and ethnic Tibet.

The Cultural Revolution

The Cultural Revolution which hit China in 1966 only worsened the situation in Tibet. The Red Guards, Tibetan as well as Chinese, destroyed every vestige of the old regime. Monasteries, castles, books, statues, paintings, chortens, and all traces of 'superstition' were savagely smashed to pieces. As in China, denunciations, torture and executions followed one another down through the years, and isolated rebellions were drowned in blood. The Cultural Revolution affected every region of Tibet, even the distant, desolate west; the artistic treasures of the ancient kingdom of Guge were destroyed.

In 1964 the Panchen Lama was accused of being an enemy of the people, of the Party, and of Socialism. For fifteen days he endured a session of public 'criticism', the violence of which heralded the Cultural Revolution (left). This began in 1966, transformed Tibet into a mass of ruins, (above, Ganden Monastery), and shattered the majority of pious Tibetans, who were forced against their will to help in the destruction of the monasteries and their contents.

The monasteries, 'nests of reactionaries and superstitions' which had survived the invasion, were systematically wiped out – often dynamited – and their contents smashed. The most valuable were sent to Beijing, where they were melted down, although in 1983, 26 tonnes of relics were discovered hidden in the Forbidden City. Of the 6,000 temples and monasteries that had existed in Tibet before 1959, practically nothing remained by 1976. A culture had been physically defiled and destroyed. Just a few Tibetans, defying all the risks, managed to hide some statues and books by burying them and transforming the temples into barns.

From 1969 onwards, people's communes were set up, and collectivization finished in 1975. Privacy disappeared. Instead of the traditional crop of barley, wheat had to be grown and harvested annually. Since the army were given priority use of all cereal crops, there was more famine amongst the civilian population.

In 1969, the bloody Nyemo rebellion was led by a woman, Trinley Chödron. She was captured and publicly executed in Lhasa, along with other partisans.

Finally, in 1975 the Chinese government introduced a policy for Han Chinese to immigrate to Central Tibet. Amdo and part of Kham – integrated with the Chinese provinces of Gansu, Qinghai, Sichuan and Yunnan – were already mixed, but the Tibet Autonomous Region was not. Now thousands of Chinese began to arrive. Statistics are incomplete, non-existent or doctored, and so it is difficult to give precise figures, but one official estimate suggests that 96,000 Han Chinese – not including military personnel – entered Central Tibet after 1982. The city of Lhasa was no longer recognizable. At the same time it is estimated that more than a million Tibetans, including those in Amdo and Kham, died between 1951 and 1976. The 13th Dalai Lama's prediction had come true.

During this period, guerrilla warfare was still being waged from the Mustang region, a Tibetan enclave in Nepal. It only ended in 1974, when the American and Nepalese governments withdrew their aid to these, the last freedom-fighters, some of whom killed themselves in despair.

A taste of liberty, 1979–87

In 1978 Deng Xiaoping received the Central Committee's backing to begin reforms. This was a new chapter in the post-Mao era. The Tibetans began to notice changes, particularly when the General Secretary of the Communist Party, Hu Yaobang, toured Tibet in 1980 and had the courage to criticize the colonialist policy of the past and the mistakes that the Chinese had made in Tibet. On seeing the poverty of the Tibetans, he could have wept for shame, and he set in motion a series of targeted economic measures, advocated autonomous decision-

The Chinese opened schools in Tibet, but all the teaching was done in Chinese, and of course the propaganda shows young girls immersed in Chairman Mao's *Little Red Book* (below). During the 1960s, many young Tibetans were sent to China to study and be indoctrinated. When they returned, they expected to be given positions of responsibility, but in fact they were sent to remote areas in order to gain 'revolutionary experience', where they remained until the end of the 1970s. These young people had hoped for a Tibet in which they could play an active role, and so were disappointed to see that China was only interested in ideological education and the class struggle, rather than the economic development of Tibet. With the creation of the Tibet Autonomous Region in 1965, 'former peasants' were promoted to administrative positions, but since they were illiterate in both Chinese and Tibetan, they were assisted by 'Party work teams' that were made up of Chinese officials.

making for the Tibetans, and decided that 85 per cent of the Chinese officials should leave the country. Prisoners were released, and the Tibetan language was once more taught in schools. In 1982, article 35 of the Chinese Constitution guaranteed freedom of worship, provided it did not endanger order and the State. Monasteries were rebuilt, and monks began to study

In effect it was not until 1980 that there was any improvement in the situation. Emphasis was then laid on economic development and on giving increased responsibility to Tibetan officials. Many projects

again. Tibet was opened to foreigners, and the University of Lhasa was created in 1985.

But in Tibet and Beijing, the Party faithful were vehemently opposed to this open policy, and Hu was deposed in January 1987. The deposing of Hu Yaobang and the mysterious death of the 10th Panchen Lama signalled the end of the one period of relative liberalization that Tibet had experienced since 1959.

Internationalization and riots

The Chinese realized that not only had they failed to crush the Tibetans, but also that Tibetan nationalism was a reality. The paradox was that they had succeeded in creating a unified opposition to themselves among Tibetan peoples who, from a political point of view, had

were launched to improve the infrastructure, using mainly female Tibetan workers (above). Tibet was opened up both to investment and to the first influx of Chinese traders. Tourism was seen as a source of revenue for the region, but proved a double-edged sword for the Chinese, because it helped to publicize the Tibetan cause internationally.

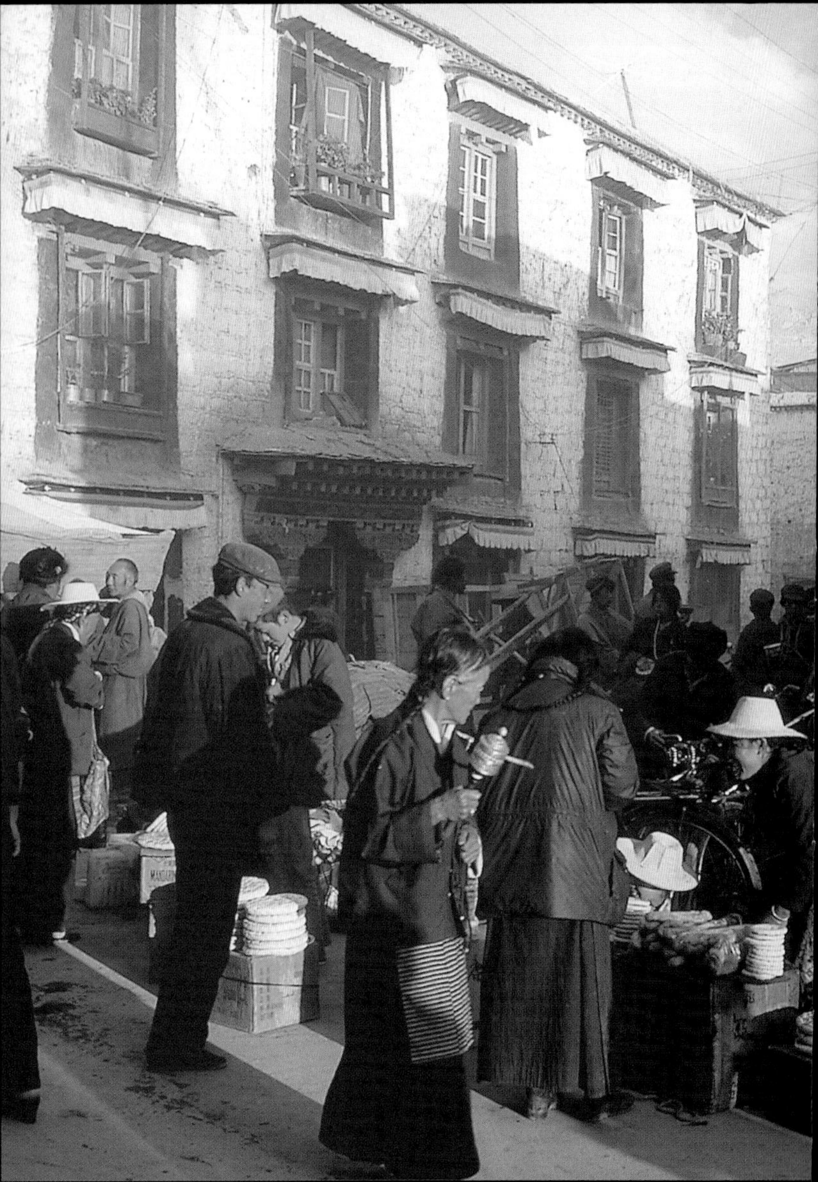

During the 1980s, the economy was liberalized and the Tibetans, who consumed 90 per cent of what they produced, were encouraged to develop a market economy. The first Chinese Muslim market-gardeners (the Hui) arrived and took over most of the trade in fresh products. In towns like Lhasa (left), nomads and Tibetan peasants sold their wares: bread, butter, vegetables. Religious practices were revived, and people gathered round the principal temple in Lhasa, the Jokhang, selling foodstuffs and holding their prayer wheels. The 10th Panchen Lama, who was compelled to renounce his monk's vows and to take a Chinese wife, returned to Tibet in 1982, where he was greeted with respect and affection (above).

not always been on the best of terms. The nuns and monks were the spearhead of this nationalism, and Buddhism was one form of its expression.

In 1987 the Dalai Lama addressed the US Congress, and the following year he delivered his Strasbourg appeal, in which he outlined his plan for Tibet. He had abandoned the idea of independence, but asked for an association between a greater, genuinely autonomous Tibet and China, for the basic rights of Tibetans to be respected, for an end to Chinese immigration, for Tibet no longer to be used as a nuclear dumping ground, and for the creation of a peace zone. A lot of Tibetans were shocked by his abandonment of the principle of independence, and the Chinese rejected his proposals because they did not contain the one clause they deemed essential: that Tibet had always been part of China.

Nevertheless, the Dalai Lama's influence grew still further when he was awarded the Nobel Peace Prize in 1989. The Tibetan cause was taken up by a number of Westerners who were interested in Buddhism, and these included famous actors and singers. This sympathy

The 1987 riots sounded the death knell of liberalization, and brought home to the Chinese that the Tibetan people had not given in. The police manhandled the monks who were proclaiming that Tibet was a free and independent nation. The police station in front of the Jokhang was set on fire by the Tibetan crowd, and the riot was bloodily put down in full view of dozens of Western tourists. Six policemen were killed according to Chinese reports; according to Western observers six Chinese policemen and seven Tibetans were killed, and dozens were injured.

filtered through into Tibet itself. Radio programmes in Tibetan were broadcast from the West, and tourists often demonstrated their support. The Tibetan cause became international, and the Dalai Lama made his voice heard in many foreign parliaments, to the fury of the Chinese, who protested vehemently. For the world outside China, Tibetan politics and religion were once more symbolized by the Dalai Lama. The time had long passed since the British Prime Minister Neville Chamberlain was able to call this 'a quarrel in a far-away country between people of whom we know nothing.'

At the end of September 1987, a week after the Dalai Lama's speech in Washington, a series of pro-independence rallies took place in Lhasa, led initially by monks and nuns. It is clear that the welcome accorded to the Dalai Lama by such a powerful nation had sparked new hope, but this was rapidly and bloodily extinguished by the police. Nevertheless, small-scale demonstrations continued until 1989, causing increasing embarrassment to the Chinese government. After the death of the Panchen Lama, Tibetan resentment exploded and, at the beginning of March 1989, there was the biggest ever anti-Chinese demonstration in Lhasa. Conscious of the symbolism underlying this, the 30th anniversary of the rebellion in Lhasa, the Chinese took no risks. The demonstration was savagely crushed, with dozens of Tibetans killed. On 8 March 1989 martial law was imposed on the whole Autonomous Region by the new Party Secretary for Tibet, the brilliant but shrewd Hu Jintao, who today is on the verge of becoming the most powerful man in China. To the Tibetans, the massacre of March 1989 was on a par with the events that took place in Beijing's Tiananmen Square

In the course of time, the Dalai Lama became a great deal more than the 'simple monk' he once aspired to be. As political head of Tibet, he had to act directly on behalf of his people, and extend international contacts. His Nobel Peace Prize in 1989 was a slap in the face to the Chinese at a time when there were more and more demonstrations in Tibet.

In Dharamsala, the Dalai Lama took part in protests against Chinese repression (above). His charisma and his speeches calling for tolerance won over many Westerners – including non-Buddhists – to the Tibetan cause. China, however, launched vehement personal attacks against him, which alienated still further the Tibetans in Tibet.

four months later. Martial law was finally lifted at the end of April 1990

'Cutting off the serpent's head'

Since then, particularly since the 3rd Work Forum in Tibet in 1994 and the crisis concerning the 11th Panchen Lama in 1995, Chinese policy in Tibet has been characterized by religious repression, political indoctrination, increased capital investment to build the economy and the infrastructure, and the promotion of massive Chinese immigration. All these policies are interdependent, because the Chinese government see economic development as an antidote to the poison of religion, and in the middle term the Tibetans have to be demographically absorbed in the Autonomous Region just as they have been in other provinces. The Tibetan exception must be eliminated, along with separatism and the demands for restoration of annexed Tibetan lands.

A propaganda document circulated after the 3rd Forum, in typical Communist jargon, clearly articulates the policy of repression: 'As the saying goes, to kill a serpent, we must first chop off its head. If we do not do that, we cannot succeed in the struggle against separatism.... It is not a matter of religious belief nor a matter of the question of autonomy, it is a matter of securing the unity of our country and opposing separatism.... Any separatist activities and convictions must be continuously crushed, according to the law. We must heighten our vigilance, and watch out for those few who are holding to a reactionary standpoint, and who are launching vengeful counterattacks and harming our cadres at the grassroots level. They must be struck down and punished severely....' (3rd Work Forum report, 1 October 1994).

A colonial policy

In addition to its strategic geographical position, Tibet is also Asia's 'water tower'. All the great rivers of Asia have their sources here, and their upper regions cross the country: the Yangtse, the Yellow River, the Mekong, the Salween, the Irrawaddy, the Indus, the Sutlej, the Brahmaputra. Reckless deforestation in the south-eastern

The image above symbolizes Chinese Tibet, on two levels. The Chinese would see it as showing the harmony between the army and the people, as they watch a religious ceremony together. But what is striking is the presence of the Tibetan and Chinese soldiers in the foreground, relaxing in their chairs, while the ordinary people stand or sit on the ground.

regions of Tibet (Kongpo and Kham) has massively eroded the soil and increased the risk of violent floods throughout South and South-East Asia, as well as on the Chinese plains. Even though a partial ban was placed on deforestation in December 1998, the exploitation continues with the active participation of the army. In forty years, forested areas throughout Tibet are estimated to have declined from 25.2 million hectares to 13.57 million, and 18 million m³ of timber have been transported from south-eastern Tibet to China. In the same period, the Chinese have given a figure of 54 billion US dollars earned through timber taken from the Autonomous Region alone.

Furthermore, the postures of the soldiers – legs stretched out or crossed, one of them reading – shows no respect for the masked dancer, who represents a fearsome deity. The irony of the spectacle is that his task is to castigate the enemies of religion with his sword. Religion has been reduced to folklore – a mere show devoid of its ritual meaning.

Tibet is also rich in minerals: gold, uranium, coal, copper, chromium, mica, borax, iron, zinc and lithium, of which it has the second largest reserves in the world. But for the moment it is too difficult and too costly for these resources to be exploited, with the exception of gold. Potential hydroelectric resources are enormous: 250,000 MW, or 57 per cent of China's potential, and power stations have been built in order to export electricity, primarily to China's paddy fields.

In this fragile ecology, with poor soil and a harsh climate everywhere except in the south-east, the soil of Tibet cannot at present sustain high yields or intensive farming. Even though the country is sparsely populated, any demographic influx would pose great dangers to an ecosystem already undermined by deforestation, soil erosion, the disappearance of some species of animals, hunted for their commercial value, and in the north of Tibet, nuclear waste.

This is a colonial economy, exploiting the riches of the country not for the benefit of the Tibetans but for that of the Chinese, and this is confirmed by the number of

Ancient buildings were demolished, and new blocks were put up with no regard for traditional architecture. Broad streets open the way for wind and dust; inelegant buildings of concrete and glass are totally unsuited to the weather conditions; the modern plumbing should have been beneficial, but the water supply is irregular; rubbish is only collected occasionally; at 7 a.m. Beijing time, which is still nighttime in Tibet, loudspeakers greet the new day in military fashion. This is modern Tibet, Chinese style (below).

Tibetan officials in positions of responsibility within the TAR: only 34 per cent of jobs at prefectorial level and above are occupied by Tibetans, and only 16 per cent in the armed forces. Furthermore, not one Communist Party Secretary in the Autonomous Region has ever been Tibetan.

The current situation

The Dalai Lama's doctrine of non-violence has been opposed since 1988 by some Tibetans who believe that middle-of-the-road pacifism simply doesn't work, especially since all attempts at negotiating with the Chinese have proved futile and have so far brought not the slightest relief to the Tibetan people. The Chinese media and officialdom now more than ever condemn the Dalai Lama as a 'separatist', and any allusion to the situation in Tibet by a foreign power is dismissed as interference in the internal affairs of China. The Chinese know that after 45 years, they still have not won the hearts of the Tibetans. Any untoward event is perceived as a violation of Party policy and is attributed to the Dalai Lama's 'clique': in 1995 the chosen reincarnation of the 10th Panchen Lama, who had died in 1989; in 1997 the publication of the secret 1962 report by the Panchen Lama; in December 1999, the flight to India of

In Chinese, Tibet is called *Xizang*, or 'Western Treasure House'. These 'treasures' include minerals, hydraulic power and forestry. The deforestation of eastern Tibet has been an environmental disaster (above, Serthar, eastern Tibet), as it has increased flooding in the Chinese plains. Tibet also contains huge uninhabited spaces, which China lacks, and these offer much scope for nuclear research. The '9th Academy' was established in the 1960s for this purpose in Qinghai, near Lake Kokonor; it has since been closed, but the untreated radioactive waste has polluted the region. However, no nuclear tests have ever been carried out in Tibet.

the young Karmapa, head of the Karma Kagyu school, who until then had been a political puppet of the Chinese.

Sometimes the Chinese government is so desperate to maintain total control over everything that the situation becomes absurd. The current situation includes a Communist state giving itself the right to recognize reincarnated lamas. The 11th Panchen Lama, Gedun Choekyi Nyima, recognized by the Dalai Lama in Tibet, disappeared in 1995, and was replaced by a Panchen Lama chosen by the Chinese. The disappearance of the Tibetan child, six years old at the time, makes him the youngest political prisoner in the world. He has not been seen for seven years, but the Chinese government assures everyone that he is well.

On 24 October 2001, addressing the European Parliament in Strasbourg, the Dalai Lama renewed his appeal for negotiations in the interests of both Tibet and China: 'I have led the Tibetan freedom struggle on a path of non-violence and have consistently sought a mutually agreeable solution of the Tibetan issue through negotiations in a spirit of reconciliation and compromise with China.... My proposal... envisages that Tibet enjoy genuine autonomy within the framework of the People's

The disappearance of the 11th Panchen Lama, recognized in Tibet by the Dalai Lama in 1995, and the fact that no foreign delegation or UN representative has ever been able to meet him – in spite of repeated demands to do so – have provoked much anger among human rights campaigners. The Chinese government merely says that the child and his parents are in good health, but it will not provide details or photographs. The boy is now aged fourteen, but the only photograph of him was taken in the year of his recognition, when he was six (above).

Republic of China. However, not the autonomy on paper imposed on us fifty years ago in the 17-Point Agreement, but a true self-governing, genuinely autonomous Tibet, with Tibetans fully responsible for their own domestic affairs, including the education of their children, religious matters, cultural affairs, the care of their delicate and precious environment, and the local economy. Beijing would continue to be responsible for the conduct of foreign and defence affairs. This solution would greatly enhance the international image of China and contribute to her stability and unity – the two topmost priorities of Beijing – while at the same time the Tibetans would be ensured of the basic rights and freedoms to preserve their own civilization and to protect the delicate environment of the Tibetan plateau.'

Even if Tibet prior to 1950 was a society in need of profound reform, was there really no other means than the destruction of a culture and the subjugation of a nation by a foreign armed force and ideology? The drawing below, by a child who lived in Tibet, is a poignant illustration of parents being separated from their children so that the latter may receive a Tibetan education in exile.

Violated rights and economic integration

Religious repression and the campaign of reeducation are once more in full swing. The recently built Serthar Monastery in Amdo (Sichuan), under the leadership of the charismatic Khenpo Jigme Phuntsok, and containing 5,000 monks and nuns including some Chinese, was destroyed in July 2001.

NAME = Phu bu Tsering
class = V.c
Tittle = About 1984 in Tibet

On 7 March 2002, Paula Dobriansky, the US State Department's Special Coordinator for Tibetan Issues, informed Congress: 'The situation on the ground in Tibet remains grave. The State Department's annual Human Rights Report for 2001, in the section on China, clearly states that tight controls on religion and other fundamental freedoms remain serious problems. The report describes in detail widespread human rights and religious freedom abuses, including instances of arbitrary arrests, detention without public trial, torture

As for the 'second generation' Tibetans born in the West or in India, even though they are of course influenced by the way of life in their host countries, they remain deeply attached to their culture and their faith, of which they consider themselves the guardians.

in prison, and official controls over Tibetan monasteries and institutions on monks and nuns. Tibet remains China's poorest region even though China has devoted substantial economic resources to Tibet over the last twenty years. Language problems severely limit educational opportunities for Tibetan students, illiteracy rates are said to be rising, and non-urban children in some regions are chronically undernourished. Some reports suggest that privatization of health care, increased emphasis on Chinese language curriculum, and continuing Han migration into Tibet are all weakening the social and economic position of Tibet's indigenous population…'

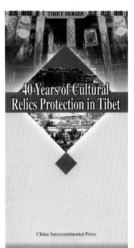

Because terror, ideology and collaboration have all failed, the Chinese government is now proceeding by means of demographic assimilation; Tibet is being populated by Chinese coming in from the 'mother country' – small traders, drivers, construction workers, and road and railway workers, not to mention the military, whose numbers are kept secret but are estimated at around 500,000, while prostitutes believed to number around 10,000. All are flocking to this inhospitable, sparsely populated country where wages are three times as high as they are in China. The government has even coined a slogan: 'Go west'. Today a railway is being constructed between Golmud, in Qinghai, and Lhasa, built by thousands of Chinese workers. It will be 1,084 km long, will cross mountain passes 5,000 m high, and will cost 2.34 billion US dollars (official figures, 1995). It is a gigantic undertaking carried out in the most testing climatic conditions, and it is due to be finished in 2007. It is 'of extreme importance to the consolidation of the south-

Mao, Deng and Jiang smile against the background of the Potala and invite Tibetans to follow them into a new era (above) – and the destruction counts for nothing in *40 Years of Cultural Relics Protection in Tibet* (left). The propaganda continues, and Chinese tourists come flocking: 404,000 in 2001 (official statistic). Foreigners require a Chinese visa and also a special permit to visit the TAR.

拉萨市政府 宣

ཀྱི་འཕྲིན་སྟོན་པ་ཡིན། ༈ ཆ་ཚོ་རྒྱས་ཐབས་གཏོང་ཞེ་ཆེན་གྱི་ཆུབས་སུ་འཁྲིད།
)领路人，带领我们走进新时代。

west frontier of the mother country, for the exploitation of the natural resources along the route, and for the establishment of direct economic and political links between Tibet and other parts of the country' (5th Development Plan of the Tibet Autonomous Region).

In 2002 a 35-metre high monument was constructed in front of the Potala, to the glory of the People's Liberation Army; the town itself is dominated by the new public security building. Thus the ancestral fear of the 'Barbarians from the West', shared by all Chinese governments since the Eastern Zhou dynasty (8th–3rd centuries BC), would seem for the moment to have been allayed.

A half-smile: in late June 2002, the Dalai Lama visited Prague, and received a portrait of himself from Vaclav Havel.

DOCUMENTS

Travellers in Tibet

'In the whole history of exploration, there is no more curious map than that which shows the tangled lines of traveller's routes towards this city (Lhasa), coming in from all sides, north, south, east and west, crossing, interlocking, retracing, all with one goal, and all baffled, some soon after the journey had begun, some when the travellers might almost believe that the next hill would give them a distant glimpse of the golden roofs of the Potala.'

Perceval Landon, 1904

Great piety

The Jesuit Antonio de Andrade (1562–1607) travelled across the whole of Central Asia and in 1626 established the first church in Tibet at Tsaparang, in the kingdom of Guge.

It is because of this piety and this inclination towards the things of God that they continually ask for crosses and reliquaries which they like to hang around their necks. The mother of the king lives in a different country which is two days' journey away from here; even before speaking to me, she sent someone to ask me for some holy object of this order. I sent her a cross and a reliquary, which gave her great pleasure. In addition to a golden cross, the king himself wears round his neck our rosary which also bears the sacred cross, and a gold reliquary with two of our relics inside. I took theirs away from them and burned them.

…It is out of pure piety as well as their good nature that they also worship our images with such devotion. We have several in this church, which is very well furnished. All the nobles and many ordinary people come flocking to it; they prostrate themselves upon the ground three times, as is their custom, and they worship the sacred images and ask for the Holy Bible to be placed on their heads; in this way we have plenty of opportunities to explain the mysteries of the faith to them.

…The opportunity arose for the king to watch us offering Holy Communion at mass. He returned to the house a few days later, and asked to see the Host again. I showed him one, broke it, and put it in his hand, saying: 'At the moment, Sire, it is only bread. But when one offers it to God, by the force of the words that He Himself taught us, it changes into his own body.' – 'Well,' he replied, 'since at the moment it is only bread, give me permission to eat it.' He took a tiny piece, and divided the rest among his servants who were present, just like someone handling a relic, a very sacred thing.

Antonio de Andrade, 1626
taken from *Les Portugais au Tibet, les premières relations jésuites (1624–1635)*, ed. Hugues Didier, Paris, 1996

On the Buddhist Trinity

Francisco de Azevedo (1578–1660) was also a member of the Tsaparang mission, which he joined in 1631. His interpretation of the Buddhist trinity – the Buddha, Buddhist law and the community of monks – is very interesting.

These people are clothed in coarse woollen tunics and breeches of the same material, with boots, the men as well as the women. They wear nothing on their heads, and wear their hair in little tresses that fall down their backs and are carefully coated with butter; for jewelry they wear amber or coral chains around the neck or on the chest. They are all as dirty as one another. From the forehead to the middle of the head falls a cord in which are threaded some rough green stones called turquoises. But some of them are beautiful. They eat meat which is either raw or barely cooked, flour made from roasted barley, and cooked vegetables. They have fresh ones all year, because during the summer they dry them at home in the shade. When they want to eat them fresh and green, all they have to do is soak bunches of them in water for half a day. Thus they are as fresh as if they had just been picked. If these are served to you, the menu is not bad.

…They believe that God is threefold. They call Him Conja Sumbo [*C'os dkon gsum pa*]. They call the Father Lama Conjo [*bLa ma dkon mc'og*], the Son Cho Conjo [*C'os dkon mc'og*], the Holy Spirit Giundu Conjo [*dGe dun dkon mc'og*]. They believe that the Father begat the Son in accordance with His word, and that the Holy Spirit was born of them both. They call Our Lady Gelobo Lunze [*Ses rab p'a rol tu p'yn pa*]. They believe that the Son is incarnated in her. God had wanted to send her an angel as His envoy, but the latter had caused much resentment among the men because they considered that in this manner he had touched her. And so God, in order to prevent disputes, had sent an elephant as his envoy. At least that is what is written in their book.

Francisco de Azevedo, 1631
taken from *Les Portugais au Tibet, les premières relations jésuites* (see above)

At Tashilunpo monastery

George Bogle (1746–81), a keen young man with great respect for local customs, wrote an excellent description of life in Tashilunpo Monastery, and the mutual curiosity with which Tibetans and Westerners regarded each other.

'From the day of our arrival at Teshu Lumbo till the 18th of January, 1775, the [Panchen] Lama was engaged in receiving visits and presents. Among the rest of his votaries were a large caravan of Kalmuks, who offered up to his shrine talents of silver, furs, pieces of silk, and dromedaries. They remained about a month at Teshu Lumbo, and then proceeded to Lhasa....

I was not present on any of these occasions, but remained at home, where I had enough visitors of my own; for crowds of *gylongs* [monks] used to come into my room to see me at all hours, or get upon the leads and look down upon

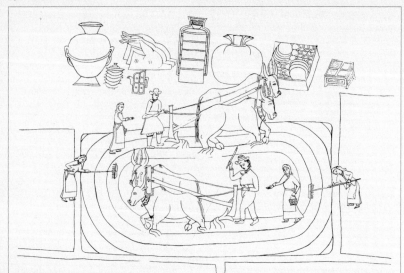

me. Among these last came the Shigatzé Killadars, dressed in their feminine attire. I never forbade anybody; and after giving them a pinch of snuff and indulging them with a look at the chairs, &c., which always produced an exclamation of "Pah-pah-pah, tze-tze-tze!" they used to retire and make way for others. This continued, more or less, all the time I was at Teshu Lumbo....

The priest, who every morning came to me with boiled rice and tea from the Lama, was called Debo Dinji Sampu. He was about fifty, marked with the smallpox, his eye mild and candid, and himself of great singleness of mind and simplicity. He came to understand my imperfect attempts to speak the Tibetan language tolerably well, and we used to have long chats together. I grew very fond of him, and he, which showed his sagacity, took a great liking to me. He always kept a box of excellent snuff, and was not niggardly in offering a pinch of it. But with all Debo Dinji's good

qualities, he was as averse to washing his hands and face as the rest of his countrymen. He happened one morning to come in while I was shaving, and I prevailed upon him for once to scrub himself with the help of soap and water. I gave him a new complexion, and he seemed to view himself in my shaving glass with some satisfaction. But he was exposed to so much ridicule from his acquaintances, that I never could get him to repeat the experiment.'

George Bogle, 1775
taken from *Narrative of the Mission of George Bogle to Tibet and of the journey of Thomas Manning to Lhasa*, ed. Clements R. Markham, London, 1879

The battle of Kuru

Perceval Landon (1869–1927), a reporter for The Times*, accompanied the British expedition to Tibet led by Colonel Francis Younghusband in 1904. His poignant description of the battle of Kuru and his* *dispatches from Lhasa stunned and thrilled his readers.*

By this time the storm had broken in full intensity, and from three sides at once a withering volley of magazine fire crashed into the crowded mass of Tibetans. It was like a man fighting with a child. The issue was not in doubt, even from the first moment; and under the appalling punishment of lead, they staggered, failed and ran. Straight down the line of fire lay their only path of escape. Moved by a common impulse, the whole mass of them jostling one against another with a curious slow thrust, they set out with strange deliberation to get away from this awful plot of death. Two hundred yards away stood a sharply squared rock behind which they thought to find refuge. But the Gurkhas from above enfiladed this position and the only hope they had lay in reaching the next spur half a mile away. Had we been armed with their weapons, another hundred yards would have brought them into safety, even in the open. It was an awful sight. One watched it with the curious sense of fascination which the display of unchecked power over life and death always exerts when exercised. Men dropped at every yard. Here and there an ugly heap of dead and wounded was concentrated, but not a space of twenty yards was without its stricken and shapeless burden. At last, the slowly moving wretches – and the slowness of their escape was horrible and loathsome to us – reached the corner, where at any rate we knew them to be safe from the horrible lightning storm which they had themselves challenged.

All this was necessary, but none the less it sicked those who took part in it, however well they realised the fact.

This was no fighting in the usual sense of the word. As soon as their first assault had failed there was nothing for the Mission escort to fear except, perhaps, the bullets of their own companions....

As I have said, Lhasa would remain Lhasa were it but a cluster of hovels on the sand. But the sheer magnificence of the unexpected sight which met our unprepared eyes was to us almost a thing incredible. There is nothing missing from this splendid spectacle – architecture, forest trees, wide green places, rivers, streams and mountains, all lie before one as one looks down from the height upon Lhasa stretching out at our feet.... The beauty of Lhasa is doubled by its utter unexpectedness... there was nothing – less perhaps in such maps and descriptions of Lhasa as we had than anywhere else – to promise us this city of gigantic palace and golden roof, these wild stretches of woodland, these acres of close-cropped grazing land and marshy grass, ringed and delimited by high trees or lazy streamlets of brown transparent water over which the branches almost met....

Lamaism may be an engine of repression, but its victims do not protest; and there before one's eyes at last is Lhasa. It may be a barrier to all human improvement; it may be a living type of all that we in the West have fought against and at last overcome, of bigotry, cruelty and slavery; but under the fierce sun of that day and the white gauze of the almost unclouded sky of Lhasa, it was not easy to find fault with the creed, however narrow and merciless, which built the Potala palace and laid out the green spaces at its foot. In this paradise of cool water and green leaves, hidden away among the encircling snows of the highest mountain ranges in the world,

Lamaism has upraised the stones and gold of Lhasa, and nothing but Lamaism could have done this thing. To Lamaism alone we owe it that when at last the sight of the farthest goal of all travel burst upon our eyes, it was worthy, full worthy, of all the rumour and glamour and romance with which in the imaginings of man it has been invested for so many years.'

Perceval Landon, 1904
taken from *Lhasa: an Account of the Country and People of Central Tibet and of the Progress of the Mission Sent There by the English Government in the Year 1903-4*, London, 1905

Dances at Patong

The French explorer Jacques Bacot (1877–1965) never succeeded in reaching Central Tibet, but his travels in the border regions of Tibet gave him an intimate knowledge of the customs, which he described in colourful style.

Yesterday evening, at the twilight hour, after we had had a good laugh at the crude or naive clowning, the festivities ended with the song of *Om mani padme*. While the three oldest men of Panong threw fistfuls of grain to the spirits of the four cardinal points, the entire crowd – men and women – started singing. Mystic syllables, whose meaning scholars search for in vain; but a magnificent sound with its fullness and its aching melody, with the voices rising very high, as high as hope can rise, and then falling again in disappointment and a profound lamentation. No one knows who composed this song, but it is without the artifice of composition. It is the work of centuries and of a whole nation, a synthesis, the very cry of human distress and hope, despairingly and eternally uttered from the depths of the abyss. It

sums up all of the Tibetan religion, and all religions.

Jacques Bacot
taken from *Le Tibet révolté*, Paris, 1912.

My adventures in the land of France

Ardjroup Gumbo (died 1910) gives a Tibetan traveller's view. He went to France with Jacques Bacot, and observed and compared French and Tibetan societies with directness and gentle humour. In his book Le Tibet révolté *(1912) Bacot, whom Gumbo called Ta-jen (master), pays homage to him: 'I owe to him feelings that people of our time no longer know and perhaps will no longer understand.'*

…I went out to visit Marseilles. On a mountain nine storeys high there is a large church; to climb this mountain there are several sorts of path. As for me, in order to climb it I entered a little house at the foot of the mountain [the lift that goes up to Notre-Dame de la Garde], and saw some men sitting down. In the time it takes to utter a cry, the house was transported to the top of the mountain and the doorway to the church. In this church there were statues of saints and virgins. At the sight of them I rejoiced and knelt down to pray. Having come up in a vehicle, we went down again to the foot of the mountain.

When we arrived at an arm of the sea, a lot of men were standing in a house suspended above the water [the transporter bridge]. And this house crossed the space above the water. We came back into town in a vehicle, and a lot of men were looking at me.

…In the inn there were more than eight storeys and a hundred rooms.… In these rooms were beds that had been made, covered with silken fabrics, and also tables loaded with ornaments. Silken fabrics without any grime covered these tables. In the evening, so that we could sleep some servants stretched the beds out, and in the morning they folded them up.

I ate with the masters of the inn at a round table. The custom in the morning is to eat a small meal of milk, coffee, butter and sugar. At midday and in the evening, there are two big meals of meat, fish, fruit and sweet things.

Before having these meals, one must wash one's body and hands, and shake the dust from one's clothes. And when I go home to my country, when I say, contemptible dog, that I am following this custom, all the men will be incredulous and will stop their ears.

Before entering the house, one must wipe one's feet on woven carpets. Not everyone is allowed in. At the main door there is a guard. First you must approach the guard, and he lets some in and not others. If he says yes, he accompanies you into the house... On every floor there are little wheels, and if you turn them a quarter turn, they give light, water, heat, everything you want; and you do not need oil or fire. I did not know how it was done, but when I looked closely I saw that underneath the house, in the earth, there was a great fire and an abundance of water.

...There is a large room where people only go to eat meals. The men eat with the women, all mixed together at a round table. In order to enter the room, the men link arms with the women and bow to them. The French like women very much, bow to them deeply, and when they talk to them, they have smiling faces and their voices are full of sweetness.

...The Ta-jen has a large country house in addition to his house in Paris... This house is as big as a fortress and is built on a little mountain. But the Ta-jen is not the chief of the country, because in France those who live in palaces have become the subjects of their farmers. The poor have become powerful, having been elected by the people, and have left their goods to the rich. But now they are beginning to want them back.

Everywhere in this house there are paintings, depicting trees, the water of lakes and rivers, gardens and fields such as one sees in the country. In these paintings there is not one god or saint to be seen, because they have not been done by priests but by clever men. And French people like looking at these paintings inside their houses.

...For three months I suffered a lot, because the cook disliked me. This female cook had a moustache; she was dirty, nasty, and did not fear God. She gave me my food as if I was a dog. After three months the Ta-jen drove her out of the house....

I've seen other bad women, but their husbands were good. In France, when a married woman has committed adultery, her husband does not kill her, as a virtuous husband must do in Tibet and China, but he goes peacefully about his affairs while everybody laughs at him and mocks him....

Ardroup Gumbo
taken from 'Impressions d'un
Tibétain en France', in Jacques Bacot,
Le Tibet révolté (see above)

A Tibetan perspective

Trade was dependent on great caravans transporting goods between the regions. These were major expeditions which lasted for months and had to protect themselves against wild animals and bandits.

Every morning, with great precision, the enormous machine got itself ready to depart: everyone got up very early, two or three hours before daybreak, at the moment when the night was at its coldest, when it was freezing enough to split stones. While the cook did what he could to heat the water for tea, the teamsters harnessed the horses. Only then did they set about loading the yaks and dismantling the camp. Every move was calculated: they needed two men per animal; it took them half an hour to load forty. They began with the animals that would be leaving first – those which had spent the night closest to the track. It was the head teamster who would decide the day before which of the yaks would go at the head of the caravan – whichever was the best; it would be constantly under surveillance, and he would guard it with his life against accidents and bandits, if necessary. The honour of the head teamster depended on it and so, by extension, the fate of all the other men.

When the caravan moved off in the morning, everything had to be done at speed in order to keep up with the front of the column, but also not to keep the rear of the column waiting. Faster! Faster! This was the constant cry that reverberated the length of the caravan and had the men complaining. Having had enough of being told that he must go faster, one of the men would sometimes do the opposite of what the master had ordered. It only needed one man to disobey, and the effect would be felt by the whole caravan. As soon as twenty yaks had been loaded, they would set off without waiting, accompanied by a teamster on horseback; then there would be another teamster accompanying twenty more yaks, then another, until finally the head teamster would set off with the last twenty yaks. Each group that followed would wait until its predecessor had departed. There was never a gap in the long line. It took an hour for the circle finally to unwind and for the whole caravan to be on the move. The last group could always sleep an hour longer than the first, and so each group took it in turns to take the lead.

That was the caravan: always in a hurry, always needing to go faster, always exciting; and yet the caravan was slow; it set off in the morning at about 5 a.m., and stopped around midday after seven hours on the move. How far did it travel each day? Fifteen to twenty kilometres.

...On its journey the caravan crossed land that belonged to different tribes of nomads; the caravan had long since made agreements with them, and every year the traders exchanged tea for skins and wool. If the caravan was simply crossing the land without trading, it would pay a toll. Most of the time there was nothing to fear – not even from the Gologs, who also needed tea. It was always the head of the caravan who negotiated with the nomad chiefs.

...In the desert, which looks completely empty, the smallest clod of earth has its own peculiarities, and the head of the caravan is first and foremost a man who knows the country; this place is good for camping because it's sheltered from the wind; the water is bad here because it comes from peat bogs; over there you'll find fuel; careful, this is a valley where you're likely to be attacked by bandits; there's the rock you have to climb to spot an ambush in the distance; this is the hollow where you can defend yourself against an attack.

The camp leader had a troop of horsemen at his disposal, changing each day; they would take it in turns to leave their duties with their respective groups, and would be designated as 'guards'. The leader would then have them under his command as a separate unit, and he would know each one by reputation. The risks would vary according to the day's itinerary. There were some stages of the journey where the countryside was open and one could see everything coming from afar. On those days the camp leader knew that he did not need the best of the guards. But there were other days when the area to be crossed was dangerous: it might be a broad, peaceful valley, but the leader knew that

often stopping to examine prints in the ground; 'So many riders passed this way yesterday; judging by their number, their direction, the weight of their mounts, they were hunters.' These advance riders were able to decide where to pitch camp. Some time before reaching the stopping place, they would be joined by the troop of men sent on by each group to set up the camp and tighten the ropes before the yaks arrived.

Other horsemen escorted the caravan en route. They protected its flank by

the only route the caravan could take was a narrow track, squeezed between the foot of the mountain and the marshes. It was from the neighbouring valley four years previously that the Gologs had mounted their attack. On such days, the camp leader appointed his best men to be guards; he knew them all, even if they did not belong to his own people.

Every morning, well before the departure of the great caravan, a small group of six to eight horsemen would leave early; they too had to be top men. Their task was to clear the road about two hours in advance of the caravan. Always in twos, they advanced along the crests from one side of the valley to the other. They reconnoitred all the valleys,

staying on higher ground. They were very independent, always galloping ahead, behind, to the sides, climbing to the tops of the hills, disappearing into the distance, always in pairs, patrolling the neighbouring valleys. Last thing in the evening, the camp leader would station the nightwatchmen on the ridges, overlooking the great circle in which the caravan spent the night.

From Samten Karmay and Philippe Sagant, *Les neuf forces de l'homme*, Nanterre, 1998.

Poetic songs

'The Tibetan language is extremely well adapted to poetic creation… because it allows the insertion of syllables without any real meaning into the body of the text, and permits some grammatical connections to be omitted in order to change the rhythm… Moreover, the Tibetans have always loved to sing, dance and shout at and to one another, and compete in verbal jousts. People of words, they have always valued language: from infancy they are still lulled to sleep by the mantras their mothers recite, or by the fabulous tales of King Gesar that are sung by the bards. Poetry is the offspring of this ambiance of song.'

Françoise Robin, *Action Poétique 157, Tibet aujourd'hui*, 1999.

The anonymous Saga of Gesar is a long sequence of thousands of verses, and has been put together over several centuries. Sung by bards who specialize in particular chapters, it is extraordinarily popular.

Instructions from Ma-ne-ne to Jo-ru

The song is *a-la tha-la tha-la tha-la*, that is the way that a speech is fashioned. *A-la* is the beginning of the speech. *Tha-la* is the way of expressing a word. And now, Jo-ru, divine son, listen to the song which I, your aunt, sing to you. In the furrows of the field in a sheltered valley, the blue-green shoots have sprouted; If the field is not adorned with fruits of good quality, in case of misfortune, how will the 'black heads' live? The blue leaves which feed the animals, even if they grow in quantities, are of no use. In the azure tent of the lofty sky, when the myriad stars are sparkling, if the full moon does not come to adorn them, who will lead them along the path of darkness? These constellations, like a guide through the darkness, even though they are great in number, are of no use. On the earth of the many-coloured Glin, Jo-ru has brought forth emanations of all kinds; if Jo-ru does not understand the sovereignty of the white Glin, will Jo-ru ever do good for all beings? When he is taken in by the deception of his emanations, it is like a sign of the dominance of Uncle Khro-thun.

The Saga of Gesar

Milarepa (1052–1135) was one of the greatest mystics and ascetics of Tibetan

Buddhism, and one of the founders of the Kagyupa order.

There are four great rivers
Birth, old age, disease and death.
They exist for all beings in this world,
    and none are spared.
Ah! Solitary site of the fortress of the
    Enlightenment!
High up near the glaciers live gods and
    spirits, the tower at the foot of the
    terraces is filled with benefactors.
Behind, a mountain holds out its curtain
    of white silk.
The paradisal groves thicken before.
I watch the water birds swing down
    from the mountain pass on to the
    bank of the pool.
Slaves tied to their worldly desires fill
    the earth, striving for material
    possessions.
The yogi who observes them clearly
    from the height of the precious rock,
    takes them as an example of the
    impermanence of all things.
They think of their own desires, like the
    trembling water, like the vision of a
    diseased eye.
The yogi looks on this life as the illusion
    of a dream.

*

I am a strange man, a hermit dressed
    in cotton, meditating in the months
    of summer in the snow-covered
    mountains: the Breath of new life
    cleanses all the mists of the body.
In the month of autumn, I beg for alms;
    nothing more than some barley to
    keep me in health.
In winter I meditate in the deep forests
    which protect me from the biting
    attacks of the wind.
In spring I dwell in the fields and hills
And so I free myself from phlegm and
    bile.

                              Milarepa

Drukpa Kunley, 'the divine madman' (1455–1529) belonged to the Buddhist school of Drukpa, and was one of the great family of the Gyas from whom the leaders of the Drukpa school traditionally came. However, his refusal to take established holy orders, his wanderings, his eccentric and shocking behaviour, and the songs that he used to teach the essence of faith all give him a unique place in Tantric Buddhism.

I take refuge in the quietened penis of
    the old man, dried up to the root,
    broken like a dead tree;
I take refuge in the flaccid vagina of the
    old woman, collapsed, impenetrable,
    like a sponge;
I take refuge in the warlike manhood of
    the young tiger, indifferent to death;
I take refuge in the lotus of girls, making
    them feel waves of bliss, freeing them
    from shame and inhibitions.

                    *

The lama without a disciple, the student
    without perseverance,
The pandit without an audience, the
    woman without a lover,
The farmer without a farm, the nomad
    without cattle,
The monk without discipline, the
    Gomchen without instruction,
The nun obsessed with sex, the man
    incapable of erection,
The whores running after money and
    the girls sighing for sex,
How ridiculous they are, how laughable
    they are!

                              Drukpa Kunley

The 6th Dalai Lama Tsangyang Gyatso (1683–1706) did not take monastic vows, and until his tragic death was torn between his religious duties and his love of pleasure. His simple poems are among the most beautiful in Tibetan literature.

White crane, lovely bird,
Lend me your wings!
I am not going far:
One day I shall return, through the land
    of Litang.

*

When the arrow is fired,
Its point sinks into the earth.
As soon as I saw my childhood
    companion again,
My heart was set upon her.

*

For so long I meditated
on the face of my lama,
yet nothing took form in my mind
except the features of my beloved!

*

If my mind which wanders and wanders
    again,
Thought only of the Dharma when she
    is absent,
then in just one lifetime, in just one
    body
I would become Buddha!

                        The 6th Dalai Lama

*Born in Litang, in eastern Tibet, the 7th
Dalai Lama, Kelsang Gyatso (1708–57),
was confronted by a difficult political
situation. He took refuge in spirituality
and religious practice, and devoted much
of his time to writing.*

What is the essence
Of all secret teachings?
That which benefits the mind
And frees it from illusion
The Sky of immaculate space
I thought to melt my mind in it;
The centre of the fresh, floating clouds
I thought to touch their softness.

                        The 7th Dalai Lama

*Nyoshul Khenpo Rinpoche (1932–99), an
ascetic with no affiliations, was one of the
masters of the spiritual tradition of the*
*Great Perfection (Dzogchen). Born in
Kham, he studied under the greatest lamas
of his time, and then went into exile.*

Actions and passions torment the mind
    unsparingly
Like violent waves, battering again and
    again
In this ocean, so unlike the Cycle
    without shores.
May it find the great peace that is its
    nature!

                        Nyoshul Khenpo Rinpoche

*Orgyän Dorje (born 1961) was born
in southern Tibet to a peasant family,
and worked on a literary magazine in
Tibet; he is one of the most typical of
contemporary poets.*

Untitled
Deprived of the sunlight
My body has become a block of ice
Deprived of the moonlight
What I can see is obscured in the half-
    light
What will nature grant me?
A violent rain to darken the hills and
    valleys?
A pure sky to dispel the half-light?
I wait, I wait for the response of the
    clouded mind.

An endless evening
The willows wave in all directions
The cold wind wounds my face
The troop of my companions
Disappears into the edge of the sky.
Before my eyes
Nothing remains but a broad empty
    plain
The song of yesterday mingles with the
    refuse
The radiance of smiles merges with the
    snow
At first I thought that all of this

Was nothing but one long sigh,
Now – it is one long evening, endless.

Orgyän Dorje

*Palden Gyal (1968–) was born in
Repkong in Amdo (Qinghai), and gained
a diploma at the Qinghai Institute of
Nationalities. In 1989 he went into exile
in India, then in England, and finally the
USA, where he is still pursuing his literary
career while working for Radio Free Asia.*

The Offering
Last night I passed from sleep
Into a terrifying world
Today I lost my being
I stuck a sharp dagger into my heart,
sliced off my head
And offered it, ornament of Mount
Kailash
I plunged my right hand into the head
of Magyäl Pomra
And stretched out my left hand towards
the summit of Khangka' Riwo
I offered my right foot to Lake Konokor
And dipped my left foot in Lake
Manasarovar
This whole body, so hard to obtain
Everywhere I make it my offering, seed
of my limbs.

Palden Gyal

*Born in Amdo, Gedun Chöghel
(1904–51), former monk, eclectic and
iconoclastic spirit, loved women and travel,
and was one of the line of 'mad saints'. He
called himself the 'beggar of Amdo' and
was a philosopher, poet and artist. His
critical view of lay and monastic society
earned him the hostility of the Tibetan
government, and imprisonment in 1947.*

Wherever it may be, whomever it may
be,
In Calcutta, in Nepal, in Peking
Or in Lhasa, in the land of snows,

If I observe them, all men seem to me to
behave in the same way, when they
see tea, butter and clothes.
Even those who do not like noise and
chatter, whose manners are calm and
disciplined, have no thoughts other
than those of an old fisherman.
The proud and filthy nobles like praise
and flattery, the common people like
trickery and deceit.
The young like games and the pleasures
of love, and now almost everyone
likes beer and tobacco.
People are attached to their families, but
hate and reject those of a different
origin.
To me, every human being has a nature
as brutal as an ox!
They go on pilgrimages to Tsari to
improve their reputation, they
practise the difficult mastery of heat
and cold in order to feed themselves,
they recite the words of the
Conqueror to gain some reward.
When one reflects, it seems clear that
everything is done for the profit one
can draw from it.
Sacrificial cakes, offerings of food and
drink, all those rituals that we
perform are nothing but a sumptuous
display.
Although there is no happiness, neither
in the valley nor at the top of the
mountain, we have no choice other
than to live on this earth, as in the
cowshed or in the kennel, until this
illusory body of flesh and blood
disappears.
Adzi! Such frankness may not be to
everyone's taste!

Gedun Chöphel

Tibetan Medicine

Based on Buddhist principles, this originated at the time of the kings (7th–9th centuries), and came under various foreign influences, especially Indian and Chinese. In the 12th century, Yuthok 'the Young' adapted Indian concepts to a Tibetan context in the Four Medical Tantras. *Tibetan medicine came of age in the 17th century, when Sangye Gyatso, the regent of Tibet, revised the Four Tantras and wrote a commentary,* The Blue Beryl, *illustrated with 79 paintings. In 1695, he founded the Chakpori school of medicine in Lhasa, for monks only.*

The physiological and pathological theories propounded in the Four Tantras were borrowed mainly from Indian *ayurveda*. The basic elements are the three humours (bile, phlegm and wind) which act upon the structures formed by the seven types of body tissue: chyle, blood, flesh, fatty tissue, bone, bone marrow and reproductive fluids (sperm or menstrual blood). While the anatomy of the organs is rudimentary, the system of channels through which the humours and other fluids circulate is, by contrast, described by sophisticated concepts that reflect the spiritual content of the tantras, in particular those enumerated in the *Kalachakra* tantra. Illness is defined as an imbalance of humours that can be caused by various factors: food, lifestyle, time of year, evil spirits, etc. Nevertheless, the function of medicine would be problematical if it did not also embrace the theory of absolute determinism that shows how past actions affect the destiny of the

individual (karma). Tibetan medicine also includes a concept developed earlier in the *Astanghrdaya Samhita* of Vagbhata, which states that there are three types of disease: those which are due to 'pathogenical factors of present life', and which can be cured by medical remedies or by exorcisms (in cases where the cause is evil spirits); those which manifest themselves with no apparent immediate cause and are the 'maturation of the fruit of past bad actions' (if severe, these can only be curbed by the ten virtuous practices); finally, those which are serious although their direct causes are minimal, and which combine pathogenical factors of present life with the effects of past bad actions.

In practice, the basic method of diagnosis is the taking of the pulse, which is a method borrowed from the Chinese, in addition to questioning, examination and, more rarely, study of the urine. Of the many different therapeutic methods taught in the Four

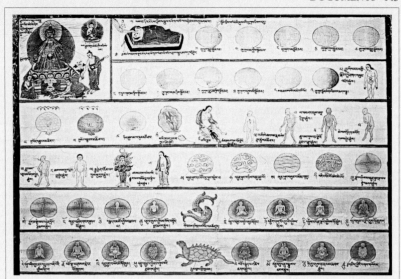

Tantras, after prescribed changes to food and lifestyle, the most commonly employed are infusions, powders and pills made up of a wide range of medicinal substances – animal, vegetable and mineral – as well as practices such as moxibustion from China.

The concepts of the Four Tantras create a 'rational' link between the biological theories inherited from Indian *ayurveda* and the foundations of Buddhist philosophy.... As the Four Tantras say, 'suffering is part of every being, even when he feels well, just as the shadow follows the bird, even though he is flying in the sky.' Tibetan medicine has not only taken up the classic comparison between the three moral poisons of Buddhism and the three humours of ayurvedic doctrine, but it has also formulated a causal link between the two.... By incorporating the three moral poisons and, ultimately, our non-cognizance of the origin of the

humours and hence of life, Tibetan medicine extends the ancient concepts of *ayurveda* in order to link them with basic Buddhist philosophy, which holds that life in all its forms is affected by mental processes, and that the chain of rebirth can only be broken through access to knowledge.

...Tibetan medicine is also closely connected with the spiritual domain both in its transmission and in its institutions.... Medical practice strictly speaking has never been clearly separated from ritual or liturgical practices – the latter being dedicated essentially to the Master Buddha of Medicine – although these are not necessarily performed by the same specialist or for the same beneficiary.

Fernand Meyer,
taken from 'Médecine et bouddhisme
au Tibet', *Grand Atlas des Religions*,
Paris, 1988

Tibet and China: the 17-Point Agreement

The Chinese government forced the Tibetan leaders to sign this document in April 1951, when the Chinese army was already in eastern Tibet. The Chinese never respected the agreement in any case, and it became a cause of disillusionment to those Tibetans who had believed in Communism. 'The Chinese authorities seem to have a short memory,' wrote a Tibetan official, 'they have forgotten what they said. Mao… announced at the time that the Chinese government would send a few soldiers and officials to help the Tibetan people and, once the situation had improved, the Chinese military and officials would immediately return to China.'

In the latter part of April, 1951, the delegates with full powers from the Local Government of Tibet arrived in Beijing. The Central People's Government appointed representatives with full powers to conduct talks on a friendly basis with the delegates of the Local Government of Tibet. The result of the talks is that both parties have agreed to establish this agreement and ensure that it be carried into effect.

1. The Tibetan people shall be united and drive out the imperialist aggressive forces from Tibet; that the Tibetan people shall return to the big family of the motherland of the People's Republic of China.

2. The Local Government of Tibet shall actively assist the People's Liberation Army to enter Tibet and consolidate the national defences.

3. In accordance with the policy towards nationalities laid down in the Common Programme of the Chinese People's Political Consultative Conference, the Tibetan people have the right of exercising national regional autonomy under the unified leadership of the Central People's Government.

4. The Central Authorities will not alter the existing political system in Tibet. The Central Authorities also will not alter the established status, functions and powers of the Dalai Lama. Officials of various ranks will hold office as usual.

5. The established status, functions and powers of the Panchen Erdeni shall be maintained.

6. By the established status, functions and powers of the Dalai Lama and the Panchen Erdeni is meant the status, functions and powers of the 13th Dalai Lama and of the 9th Panchen Erdeni when they were in friendly and amicable relations with each other.

7. The policy of freedom of religious belief laid down in the Common Programme of the Chinese People's Political Consultative Conference will be protected. The Central Authorities will not effect any change in the income of the monasteries.

8. The Tibetan troops will be reorganized step by step into the People's Liberation Army, and become part of the national defence forces of the People's Republic of China.

9. The spoken and written language and school education of the Tibetan nationality will be developed step by step in accordance with the actual conditions in Tibet.

10. Tibetan agriculture, livestock raising, industry and commerce will be developed step by step, and the people's livelihood will be improved step by step in accordance with the actual conditions in Tibet.

11. In matters relating to various reforms in Tibet, there will be no compulsion on the part of the Central Authorities. The Local Government of Tibet should carry out reforms of its own accord, and when the people raise demands for reform, they must be settled through consultation with the leading personnel of Tibet.

12. In so far as former pro-imperialist and pro-KMT* officials resolutely sever relations with imperialism and the KMT and do not engage in sabotage or resistance, they may continue to hold office irrespective of their past.

13. The People's Liberation Army entering Tibet will abide by all the above-mentioned policies and will also be fair in all buying and selling and will not arbitrarily take even a needle or a thread from the people.

14. The Central People's Government will handle the external affairs of the area of Tibet; and there will be peaceful co-existence with neighbouring countries and the establishment and development of fair commercial and trading relations with them on the basis of equality, mutual benefit and mutual respect for territory and sovereignty.

15. In order to ensure the implementation of this agreement, the Central People's Government will set up a military and administrative committee and a military area headquarters in Tibet, and apart from the personnel sent there by the Central People's Government it will absorb as many local Tibetan personnel as possible to take part in the work. Local Tibetan personnel taking part in the military and administrative committee may include patriotic elements from the Local Government of Tibet, various district and various principal monasteries; the name list is to be prepared after consultation between the representatives designated by the Central People's Government and various quarters concerned, and is to be submitted to the Central People's Government for approval.

16. Funds needed by the military and administrative committee, the military area headquarters and the People's Liberation Army entering Tibet will be provided by the Central People's Government. The Local Government of Tibet should assist the People's Liberation Army in the purchases and transportation of food, fodder and other daily necessities.

17. This agreement will come into force immediately after signatures and seals are affixed to it.

* KMT: the Kuomintang, the Chinese Communist Party

The Tibetans, the Party and the Lamas

The political problems between China and Tibet cannot simply be reduced to a conflict between the Dalai Lama and the Chinese government. Other lesser-known participants also play an important role, and religious history and the Communist Party must also be taken into account. This political issue rests on the shifting sands of historical forces, Party edicts, and the conclusions that can be drawn from these.

In 1950, true to the spirit of Mao, the Marxist view of religion as the 'opium of the people' was to be imposed, the temporal and spiritual influence of the Dalai Lama was at all costs to be undermined, and the feudal society overturned. This was the ultimate aim which nothing was to prevent, and many sectors of Chinese society, as well as some Tibetans, were totally sincere in their desire to build a new society in Tibet. The dominance of the Chinese army and party representatives, the thousands of prisoners thrown into labour camps, the famine caused by the 'great leap forward', the Cultural Revolution, the bloody repressions of the late 1980s, the death of the Panchen Lama in 1989, and the disappearance of his reincarnation in 1995, and finally the constant attacks on the Dalai Lama and the refusal by the Chinese to engage in any form of dialogue – all these destroyed the illusions of those Tibetans who had trusted the invaders.

It is true that the Tibet Autonomous Region is making some progress, at least from the point of view of economic statistics. The Chinese government and provinces are helping to improve infrastructures, telephones work, markets are well stocked and shops are bursting with goods, including the latest two-in-one shampoos. But behind the facade lie severe social problems: Tibetans who do not speak Chinese are marginalized; shops are mainly owned by the Chinese; Lhasa has the greatest number of prostitutes per head of the population of any town in Asia; alcohol and gambling are the only escape routes.

In order to endure and survive a situation in which political change is only possible by way of conflict within the Party, Tibetans have become a schizophrenic people. They profit from the economic progress, comply with political directives, and live side by side with the Chinese because they know that any open revolt will be futile given the military might of the army. They 'negotiate' their lives within the constraints of the Party line. At the same time, they laugh at themselves and their karma, despise the Chinese who are doing so well out of them (interracial marriages are rare), and no change escapes their mordant humour. They manage to keep practising their religion, with a faith that nothing can shake, and they venerate the lamas. Many are ready to make huge sacrifices to give their sons and daughters a good education, and are even prepared to be separated from their children forever in order to let them study in India. Fifty years of political instruction have simply passed them by. Their obvious resilience is matched only by their deep determination. The 10th Panchen Lama, who died in 1989, was a symbol for the Tibetan people, and the image of him as a collaborator, opposed to that of the Dalai Lama as a resistance fighter, is simplistic.

What is true, however, is that since his exile in 1959 and his Nobel Peace Prize in 1989, the Dalai Lama has become a major international figure. His charisma has united all the exiled Tibetans behind him, regardless of their religious affiliation; he also favours an ecumenical movement among the different Buddhist schools. Some of the great religious figures from his own school, the 5th and 8th Panchen Lamas, were members of Bönpo families, and today – as the 5th Dalai Lama did in the 17th century – the 14th Dalai Lama recognizes the Yundrung Bön as one of the spiritual schools of Tibet on a par with the four Buddhist schools. Although each school has its own leader – like the Karmapa, exiled in India since 2000 – the Dalai Lama is the political figure around whom they all revolve. For the vast majority of Tibetans in Tibet, after the death of the 10th Panchen Lama, he has become an object of worship – more or less covertly through fear of reprisals – as a symbol of resistance against Chinese oppression.

The matter of the 11th Panchen Lama, however, remains a burning issue. In 1642 the 5th Dalai Lama became political head of Tibet, and the religious school of Gelugpa grew in influence. In 1662, to pay homage to his master, who lived in the Tashilunpo Monastery in Shigatse, the 5th Dalai Lama established the incarnate lineage of the Panchen Lamas. But from the 6th Panchen Lama in the 18th century onwards, these became more and more independent in their relations with the Tibetan government and the Dalai Lama, and directed their sympathies towards the Qing dynasty, who played one hierarchy off against the other.

When the Chinese invaded in 1950, the young 10th Panchen Lama was in Amdo and was taken captive by the Communists. He was therefore brought up partly by the Chinese, but after 1959 remained in Tibet. His criticisms of Chinese policies in Tibet, however, cost him 18 years' imprisonment in Beijing. Having been 'rehabilitated', he returned to Tibet in 1978 and was appointed Vice-President of the Autonomous Region; as such he worked for the good of the Tibetan people despite the very strict limitations on his actions. Greatly respected, he opposed the construction of a hydroelectric dam on the sacred lake of Yamdrok Tso. He died under mysterious circumstances in 1989, at the age of 51, in Tashilunpo.

The 11th Panchen Lama was recognized by the Dalai Lama in Tibet in 1995, but the Chinese government rejected this decision, and the child disappeared, thus becoming the youngest political prisoner in the world. The Chinese government recognized a different 11th Panchen Lama, who had been brought up in Beijing and was 'in good health through the care of the Central Committee and the efforts of the different departments' (Xinhua). When he visited Tibet in June 2002, he declared that 'the changes in present-day Tibet have made me more confident in the wise governance of the Central Committee of the Party' (Xinhua).

Beyond the sad tale of a child who has disappeared, and the pronouncements made by another child of 12 who has no say in his own fate, there is a political problem in the making. Since the Dalai Lamas and the Panchen Lamas take it in turns to recognize each other's succeeding incarnations, the Chinese government will in future be in a position to allow their own Panchen Lama to recognize the reincarnation of the current Dalai Lama. The irony here is that the Communist Party, for whom religion is anathema, still discusses and decides the selection of reincarnations. The current Dalai Lama is therefore confronted now with questions of succession which, as is always the case in Tibet, are both political and religious. He has declared that the 15th Dalai Lama will be born 'in a free country'.

Françoise Pommaret

The hopes of the Dalai Lama

...Within the context of the present tense political atmosphere the Chinese authorities in Tibet have continued in the past year to subject Tibetans inside Tibet to gross violations of human rights, including religious persecution. This has led to an increasing number of Tibetans risking their lives to flee Tibet and to find refuge elsewhere. Last summer the expulsion of thousands of Tibetan and Chinese monks and nuns from a Tibetan Buddhist learning institute at Serthar in Eastern Tibet highlighted the intensity and scale of the repression in Tibet. These abuses of rights are a clear example of how Tibetans are deprived of their right to assert and preserve their own identity and culture.

I believe that many of the violations of human rights in Tibet are the result of suspicion, lack of trust and true understanding of Tibetan culture and religion. As I have said many times in the past, it is extremely important for the Chinese leadership to come to a better and deeper understanding and appreciation of the Tibetan Buddhist culture and civilization. I absolutely support Deng Xiaoping's wise statement that we must 'seek truth from facts'. Therefore, we Tibetans must accept the progress and improvements that China's rule of Tibet has brought to the Tibetan people and give recognition to it. At the same time the Chinese authorities must understand that the Tibetans have had to undergo tremendous suffering and destruction during the past five decades. The late Panchen Lama in his last public address in Shigatse on January 24, 1989 stated that Chinese rule in Tibet had brought more destruction than benefit to the Tibetan people.

The Buddhist culture of Tibet inspires the Tibetans with values and concepts of compassion, forgiveness, patience and a reverence for all forms of life that are of practical benefit and relevance in daily life and hence the wish to preserve it. Sadly, our Buddhist culture and way of life are under threat of total extinction. The majority of Chinese 'development' plans in Tibet are designed to assimilate Tibet completely into the Chinese society and culture and to overwhelm Tibetans demographically by transferring large numbers of Chinese into Tibet. This unfortunately reveals that Chinese policies in Tibet continue to be dominated by 'ultra-leftists' in the Chinese government, despite the profound changes carried out by the

Chinese government and the Party elsewhere in the People's Republic of China. This policy is unbefitting of a proud nation and culture such as China and against the spirit of the 21st century....

It is my sincere hope that the Chinese leadership will find the courage, wisdom and vision to solve the Tibetan issue through negotiations. Not only would it be helpful in creating a political atmosphere conducive to the smooth transition of China into a new era but also China's image throughout the world would be greatly enhanced. It would have a strong, positive impact on the people in Taiwan and will also do much to improve Sino-Indian relations by inspiring genuine trust and confidence. Times of change are also times of opportunities. I truly believe that one day, there will be the chance at dialogue and peace because there is no other choice for China or for us. The present state of affairs in Tibet does nothing to alleviate the grievances of the Tibetan people or to bring stability and unity to the People's Republic of China. Sooner or later, the leadership in Beijing will have to face this fact. On my part, I remain committed to the process of dialogue. As soon as there is a positive signal from Beijing, my designated representatives stand ready to meet with officials of the Chinese government anywhere, anytime. My position on the issue of Tibet is straightforward. I am not seeking independence. As I have said many times before, what I am seeking is for the Tibetan people to be given the opportunity to have genuine self-rule in order to preserve their civilization and for the unique Tibetan culture, religion, language and way of life to grow and thrive. For this, it is essential that the Tibetans be able to handle all their domestic affairs and to freely determine their social, economic and cultural development.

In exile we continue with the democratization of the Tibetan polity. Last March, I informed the elected representatives of the Assembly of Tibetan People's Deputies that the Tibetan exiles must directly elect the next Kalon Tripa (Chairman of the Tibetan Cabinet). Consequently, last August for the first time in Tibet's history, the Tibetan exiles directly elected Samdhong Rinpoche as the new Kalon Tripa by a margin of over 84 per cent of the total votes cast....

I take this opportunity to thank the numerous individuals, including members of governments, of parliaments and of non-governmental organizations who have been continuing to support our non-violent freedom struggle. It is most encouraging to note that universities, schools, religious and social groups, artistic and business communities as well as people from many other walks of life have also come to understand the problem of Tibet and are now expressing their solidarity with our cause. Similarly, we have been able to establish cordial and friendly relations with fellow Chinese Buddhists and ordinary Chinese people living abroad and in Taiwan....

Finally, I pay homage to the brave men and women of Tibet who have and who continue to sacrifice their lives for the cause of our freedom and pray for an early end to the suffering of our people.

Statement made by His Holiness The Dalai Lama on 10 March 2002 in Dharamsala, India, on the 43rd Anniversary of Tibetan National Uprising Day

THE DALAI LAMAS AND PANCHEN LAMAS

THE DALAI LAMAS

1st Dalai Lama (named retrospectively):
Gendun Drub (1391–1475)
2nd Dalai Lama (named retrospectively):
Gyalwa Gendun Gyatso (1475–1542/3)
3rd Dalai Lama: Gyalwa Sonam Gyatso
(1543–88)
4th Dalai Lama: Yonten Gyatso (1589–1617)
5th Dalai Lama: Ngawang Lobsang Gyatso
(1617–82)
6th Dalai Lama: Rigdzin Tsangyang Gyatso
(1683–1706)
7th Dalai Lama: Kelsang Gyatso (1708–57)
8th Dalai Lama: Jampel Gyatso (1758–1804)
9th Dalai Lama: Lungtok Gyatso (1806–15)
10th Dalai Lama: Tsultrim Gytso (1816–37)
11th Dalai Lama: Khedrup Gyatso (1838–56)
12th Dalai Lama: Trinley Gyatso (1856–75)
13th Dalai Lama: Thubten Gyatso (1875–1933)
14th Dalai Lama: Tenzin Gyatso (born 6 July
1935)

THE PANCHEN LAMAS

The dates differ slightly according to the source
1st Panchen Lama (named retrospectively):
Kedrup Je (1385–1438)
2nd Panchen Lama (named retrospectively):
Sonam Choklang (1439–1504)
3rd Panchen Lama (named retrospectively):
Lobsang Dondrup (1505–66)
4th Panchen Lama (the first to be named in his
lifetime): Lobsang Chögyen (1567–1662)
5th Panchen Lama: Lobsang Yeshe (1663–1737)
6th Panchen Lama: Palden Yeshe (1738–80)
7th Panchen Lama: Tenpe Nyima (1782–1853/4)
8th Panchen Lama: Tenpe Wangchuk (1854/5–82)
9th Panchen Lama: Choeki Nyima (1883–1937)
10th Panchen Lama: Choeki Gyaltsen (1938–89)
11th Panchen Lama (recognized by 14th Dalai
Lama in 1995, but since imprisoned by Chinese
government): Gedhun Choeki Nyima (1989–)
11th Panchen Lama (chosen by the Chinese
government; dubbed 'the Chinese Panchen
Lama'): Gyaltsen Norbu (1990–)

FURTHER READING

BOOKS

Adhe Taponstsang, *Ama Adhe, The Voice that
Remembers: the Heroic Story of a Woman's Fight
to Free Tibet*, Boston, 1997
Anagarika Brahmacari Govinda, *The Way of the
White Clouds: a Buddhist Pilgrim in Tibet*,
London, 1966
Ani Pachen & Donnelley, Adelaide, *Sorrow
Mountain: the Journey of a Tibetan Warrior Nun*,
London, 2000
Arpi, Claude, *The Fate of Tibet: When Big Insects
Eat Small Insects*, New Delhi, 1999
Avedon, John F., *In Exile from the Land of Snows*,
New York and London, 1985
Avedon, John F., *Tibet Today*, London, 1988.
Bacot, Jacques, *Milarepa*, Paris, 1971
Baker, Ian A. & Shrestha, Romio, *The Tibetan Art
of Healing*, London and San Francisco, 1997
Bogle, George & Manning, Thomas, *Narratives
of the Mission of George Bogle to Tibet, and of
the Journey of Thomas Manning to Lhasa*,
ed. Clements R. Markham, London, 1876
Buffetrille, Katia & Diemberger, Hildegard (eds),
Territory and Identity in Tibet and the Himalayas,
Leiden and Boston, 2002
Cornu, Philippe, *Padmasambhava*, Paris, 1997
Dalai Lama, *Freedom in Exile: the Autobiography of
the Dalai Lama*, London and Berkeley, 1990
Dalai Lama and Rowell, Galen, *My Tibet*, New
York and London, 1990
David-Néel, Alexandra, *My Journey to Lhasa*,
London, 1983 (1st ed. 1927)
David-Néel, Alexandra & Lama Yongden, *The
Superhuman Life of Gesar of Ling, the Legendary
Tibetan Hero*, trans. Violet Sidney, London, 1933
Didier, Hugues, *Les Portugais au Tibet, premières
relations jésuites*, Paris, 1996
Dodin, Thierry & Rather, Heinz (eds), *Imagining
Tibet: Perceptions, Projections, and Fantasies*,
London, 2001.

Donnet, Pierre-Antoine, *Tibet: Survival in Question*, trans. Tica Broch, London and Delhi, 1994

Fisher, Robert E., *Art of Tibet*, London and New York, 1997

Föllmi, Olivier, *Homage to Tibet*, London, 1996

Ford, Robert, *Captured in Tibet*, Hong Kong and Oxford, 1990

Goldstein, Melvyn, *A History of Modern Tibet, 1913-1951, The Demise of the Lamaist State*, Berkeley, 1989

Havnevik, Hanna, *Tibetan Buddhist Nuns: History, Cultural Norms and Social Reality*, Oslo, 1989

Heller, Amy, *Tibetan Art: Tracing the Development of Spiritual Ideals and Art in Tibet, 600–2000 AD*, Woodbridge, NY, 1999

Hergé, *Tintin in Tibet*, London and Boston, 1990

Jackson, David Paul, *A History of Tibetan Painting: the Great Tibetan Painters and Their Traditions*, Vienna, 1996

Jones Tung, Rosemary, *A Portrait of Lost Tibet*, photos by Ilya Tolstoy and Brooke Dolan, Berkeley, 1996

Landon, Perceval, *Lhasa: an Account of the Country and People of Central Tibet and of the Progress of the Mission Sent There by the English Government in the Year 1903-4*, London, 1905

Lehman, Steve, *The Tibetans: a Struggle to Survive*, London, 1999

Lobzang Jivaka, *The Life of Milarepa: Tibet's Great Yogi*, London, 1994

Lopez Jr, Donald S., *Prisoners of Shangri-La. Tibetan Buddhism and the West*, Chicago and London, 1998

Meyer, Fernand, *Gso ba rig pa. Le système médical tibétain*, Paris, 2002 (1st ed. 1988)

Nyoshul Khenpo Rinpoche & Surya Das, *Natural Great Perfection: Dzogchen Teachings and Vajra Songs*, Ithaca, NY, 1995

Palden Gyatso, *Fire under the Snow*, trans. Tsering Shakya, London, 1997

Pommaret, Françoise, *Les Revenants de l'au-delà dans le monde tibétain*, Paris, 1998 (1st ed. 1989)

Pommaret, Françoise (ed.), *Lhasa in the Seventeenth Century: the Capital of the Dalai Lamas*, trans. Howard Solverson, Leiden and Boston 2002

Rawson, Philip, *Sacred Tibet*, London and New York, 1991

Ribes, Jean-Paul, *Karmapa*, Paris, 2000

Ricard, Matthieu & Föllmi, Olivier & Danielle, *Buddhist Himalayas: People, Faith and Nature*, London and New York, 2002

Samten Gyaltsen Karmay, *The Treasury of Good Sayings: a Tibetan History of Bon*, London, 1972

Samten Gyaltsen Karmay, *Secret Visions of the Fifth Dalai Lama. the Gold Manuscript in the Fournier Collection*, Musée Guimet, Paris, London, 1998

Snelling, John *The Buddhist Handbook: a Complete Guide to Buddhist Teaching, Practice, History and Schools*, London, 1987

Stein, R. A., *Tibetan Civilization*, trans. J. E. Stapleton Driver, London, 1972

Tashi Khedrup, *Adventures of a Tibetan Fighting Monk*, Bangkok, 1986

TIN (Tibet Information Network), *Cutting off the Serpent's Head*, London, 1996

TIN (Tibet Information Network), *Leaders in Tibet*, London, 1997

Tsering Shakya, *The Dragon in the Land of Snows: a History of Modern Tibet since 1947*, London, 1999

Tucci, Giuseppe, *Tibet: Land of Snows*, trans. J. E. Stapleton Driver, London, 1967

Willis, Janice D. (ed.), *Feminine Ground: Essays on Women and Tibet*, Ithaca, NY, 1989

CD-ROM

Thurman, Robert A. F., *Illuminated Tibet*, Mystic Fire, 2000.

AUDIO CDS

Philip Glass, *Kundun*, Warner Music, 1997.

Lama Gyurme & Jean-Philippe Rykiel, *Rain of Blessings/Vajra Chants*, Real World, 2000.

Ngawang Khechog, *Quiet Mind*, Tibet Universal Music, 1991.

Tenzin Gönpo, *In Memory of Tibet*, Tshangpa, 1999.

Yangchen Lhamo, *Tibet, Tibet*, Real World, 2000.

SELECTED WEBSITES

Tibetan Government-in-Exile: www.tibet.net

Dalai Lama's official site: www.dalailama.com

Himalayan Art Project (S. & D. Rubin Foundation): www.tibetart.com

International Campaign for Tibet (USA): www.savetibet.org

Radio Free Asia: www.rfa.org

Tibet Information Network (TIN): www.tibetinfo.net

Tibetan Bulletin: tibetnews.com

China's Tibet: www.tibetinfor.com

LIST OF ILLUSTRATIONS

The following abbreviations have been used:
a above; *b* below; *l* left; *r* right

CHAPTER 5

DOCUMENTS

INDEX

PHOTO CREDITS

An anthropologist and historian, Françoise Pommaret has travelled widely in Tibet and has lived and worked in Bhutan since 1981. She has worked for the Bhutan Tourism Corporation (1981–86) and the Department of Education of the Royal Government of Bhutan, and now works as a researcher for CNRS, specializing in the history of the Tibetan region, and for INALCO, the French National Institute for Oriental Languages and Civilizations. She is the author of many books and articles of both scientific and general interest.

For S. K. and the people of Tibet

Translated from the French *Le Tibet: Une civilisation blessée*
by Barbara Mellor and David H. Wilson

First published in the United Kingdom in 2003 by
Thames & Hudson Ltd, 181A High Holborn,
London WC1V 7QX

British Library Cataloguing-in-Publication Data

A catalogue record for this book is available
from the British Library

ISBN 0–500–30112–3

Printed and bound in Italy by Editoriale Lloyd, Trieste